The Definitive Guide to Freedom from Tobacco

Quit Smoking Now and Forever! Conquering the Nicotine Demon

Helen Basinger

Quit Smoking Now and Forever - Conquering the Nicotine Demon

ISBN 978-1622-877-41-6 PRINT
ISBN 978-1622-877-42-3 EBOOK

LCCN 2014954789

November 2014

Published and Distributed by
First Edition Design Publishing, Inc.
P.O. Box 20217, Sarasota, FL 34276-3217
www.firsteditiondesignpublishing.com

"There was a young lady named Mae
Who smoked without stopping all day;
As pack followed pack,
Her lungs first turned black,
And eventually rotted away."

Edward Gorey

"Giving up smoking is the easiest thing in the world. I know because I've done it thousands of times."

Mark Twain

I dedicate this book to all the people in the world who go through addiction and come out the other side wiser and stronger.

Table of Contents

Helen Basinger is not a medical practitioner and the information in this book is not intended to diagnose or treat any medical condition, whether physical or emotional. In the event you use any of the information in this book for yourself, which is your human (and constitutional) right, the author assumes no responsibility for your actions.

When you go to the link and listen to the hypnosis session online do so in a place where you can relax and close your eyes. Driving or working would not be the right place to go into a trance!

Acknowledgments

I want to acknowledge two good men who risked everything and lost a lot, in order to expose the secret manipulations of a tobacco industry that purposely made cigarettes as addictive as possible. They are Dr. Jeffrey Wigand and Dr. Victor DeNoble – still both working tirelessly as anti-smoking advocates. God bless you both.

I want to acknowledge my friend and healer Linda Fyfe who made me aware of Elizabeth and my team on the "other-side" who have been helping me write this book. I also acknowledge John Kehoe whose brilliant book *Quantum Warrior* inspired me to add the phrases for contemplation after each chapter. A few of them are directly from him.

I also want to acknowledge my loving husband, Joel, for finally quitting, my nieces Sophie and Jessica for also seeing the light, as well as all the people who allowed me to help them finally break free from nicotine addiction.

My heartfelt thanks go to Alice Otto who did a great job editing this book. I also want to thank all the kind people who supported me in order to get this book published and to market: my mother, Sonia Tunnicliffe, Derek Tunnicliffe, Toni Guidice, Dale Alexander, Steve Shaw, Lezlie and Jim Roark, Ashley Hoyt, as well as so many other dear friends and supporters.

Author's Note

The nicotine demon works by hijacking your brain, your body, your mind; some would say, even your soul.

This dark creature surrounds you in a gray cloud where you can wander for years, sometimes not even realizing you are lost. Until for some reason, one day, you awaken and find yourself hankering after bright sunshine again.

All this time he's been fooling you into thinking you needed him – even that you liked him – while behind the scenes his dark smoky tentacles have been slowly sucking the life out of you.

In the same way that real parasites like tapeworms give off chemicals to make you desire the kind of food *they* want to eat, the nicotine demon manages to convince you that *you* are the one choosing to smoke, rather than it needing you, its host, to keep it fed.

Adopting this perspective is the first step to victory. Once you know you have a nasty parasite living inside of you, controlling you, you can't help but develop a strong urge to get rid of it. In fact I suspect you would do whatever was required to get it out of your body as fast as possible!

This book is about exposing the nicotine parasite (or nicotine demon as I like to refer to it), getting you 100% motivated to do whatever it takes, and giving you the remedy to conquer it forever.

Introduction

Bravo for deciding to quit! Bravo for deciding to kick your nicotine addiction! Bravo for choosing to be free! Bravo for having the guts to face the nicotine demon, and conquer him forever!

Going back to being a non-smoker is the best decision you will ever make, and with the help of this book and its associated content you *will* succeed.

In many ways I'm a lot like you. I used to be a smoker. I really liked it actually. I totally bought into the "cigarette in one hand, glass of wine in the other" thing. I thought I was rather sophisticated, especially with those little brown cigarillos I used to smoke during the time I lived in Paris. Then a number of things happened.

I suddenly woke up to the fact that the big global corporations and their governments were not necessarily looking out for my best interests as I had imagined. Making money, not preserving/defending human well-being or even human life, was king of kings. Also, I had passed the 40-year mark and was starting to look at ways to stay young and healthy. I did not want the wrinkles smokers get, much less the debilitating diseases and befuddled mind that could await me if I carried on. I started juicing every morning and doing yoga a couple of times a week. My interest in matters of the spirit was also reignited. Then what really amplified my resolve was the death of a close friend of 25 years. He was a heavy smoker who would still be alive today if it were not for cigarettes. He was a loving and intelligent man who would have done a lot of good if his life had not been cut short.

I was lucky in that I'd never been a heavy smoker and was one of the few who were able to put it down for good, once I made the decision. I believe I was helped by the fact that I was living in Turkey at the time, where cigarettes were free of most of the additives that are found in American cigarettes today.

Ten years later I became certified as a Master Clinical Hypnotist here in Florida. Many of my first clients naturally came to me for help with quitting smoking and I started to learn how hard it was for most people to stop. Some had tried over and over, and the nicotine demon always seemed to win.

You may be like them, and have experienced a number of unsuccessful attempts, but don't beat yourself up for failing. According to the World Health Organization fifty percent of all smokers try to quit every year, but only two and a half percent of those who try to stop without support are successful after twelve months. If that isn't bad enough, it takes that lucky minority an average of three to six attempts to get it right. Just to put that into perspective, I heard that twelve percent of heroin addicts are able to quit with no assistance.

That's an awful lot of stress, frustration, and sense of failure for a marginal success rate. The truth is, most people who are trying to quit don't have any idea what they are up against, and they are shocked at how hard it is once they actually try.

If you're serious about quitting cigarettes you need to really understand your enemy before you can put together a winning battle plan. The tobacco companies have invested billions of dollars to create a very powerful nicotine demon indeed, so you'll probably need some physical backup: stress reduction techniques, products to lessen withdrawal symptoms, and even certain foods to make the quitting easier. Most importantly you need a seasoned guide to lead you to success.

I will be that guide.

I've helped people successfully quit smoking using all kinds of methods. In my own practice, Freedom Healing, I use hypnosis for spirit release, past life regression, and instilling positive affirmations, as well as Tapping (Emotional Freedom Technique) for releasing negative emotions (including craving) and herbs to help with the physical addiction. I am also familiar with Nicotine Replacement Therapy combined with coaching as a result of my work for a free quit-smoking program called AHEC that has helped thousands of people quit smoking for good.

When working one-on-one with clients, I discovered that by using hypnosis it is possible to get someone to quit smoking quite easily. However if the issues behind the smoking are not resolved, the ex-smoker risks starting again at a future date or turning to another addiction, often food, to replace the medicating effect of cigarettes. As a result, each of my sessions – or often a series of a few sessions – now starts with an explanation of what cigarettes really are and how nicotine works, followed by a releasing of negative emotions. Then, and only then, I deliver visualizations and positive affirmations while the client is in hypnosis – which is a focused trance designed to allow their subconscious mind to experience being someone who no longer smokes.

Part of this book talks to your conscious mind and part of it talks to your subconscious mind. It's your subconscious mind that loves images and symbols and it's the one that's been preventing you from quitting up until now.

You may be someone who is naturally attracted to the idea of hypnosis, or you may not. Perhaps you are drawn to the idea of quitting with natural herbs or nicotine patches. Because everyone reading this book is different, I've included all the tools that I've seen work so that you can choose the ones that feel right for you. I'll explain nicotine replacement and the different herbs that prevent cravings. I'll teach you about homeopathy, vitamins, minerals, and nutrition that can all help you quit. I'll share visualization, affirmations, statements for contemplation, hypnosis, and Tapping techniques that will change your mental and emotional states from those of a smoker to a non-smoker. I'll outline a plan to prevent you from putting on weight once you stop smoking. Most importantly, in order to ensure your continued victory, I will give you some tools to help you let go of any issues that have prevented your success in the past

Don't be discouraged if you go off track a few times. Don't lose heart if it takes you longer than you had hoped or even if you end up having to use every trick in the book. The important thing is that you go back to being the non-smoker you were born to be, and then stay free forever.

*****

I suggest you read this book once all the way through and then re-read the daily instructions as you navigate the quitting process.

The first part of the book gives you an understanding of how cigarettes have been manipulated, and what they do to your body, mind, and spirit. Then I'll categorize and describe various cessation products and outline strategies on how to be successful. Following this, I'll walk you through a comprehensive daily plan to help keep you on track, and share advice on how to prevent you from slipping back into this powerful addiction.

Included with this book is the link to a downloadable hypnosis MP3 that I created to assist you quit. You can listen to it at www.quitsmokingnowandforever.com once you have registered for the members' page. Preferably listen to it at night before going to sleep, using headphones, and keep listening to it until you no longer smoke.

I've also made videos of the various visualizations and Tapping sessions so that you can follow along with them, rather than having to read them. They too can be found and downloaded at www.quitsmokingnowandforever.com. If it feels right, you might like to start with just the hypnosis, the breathing techniques, the visualizations, and the Tapping sessions before deciding whether you actually do need to use the physical tools.

Throughout the book I've included some powerful phrases for contemplation. Contemplation means you sit quietly for five or ten minutes and say the phrase over and over, stressing different words, allowing your mind to think about what it really means and the implication of the various parts of the statement. It is a wonderful way of expanding the mind and will really assist you in your quest for freedom from smoking.

At the end of the book I've included full instructions on how to do Tapping yourself so that you are able to release all the negative emotions which could be at the root of your smoking, and could potentially trigger you to smoke again at some point in the future.

*****

Even though the idea of quitting may make you feel nervous, know it's completely normal. Take a deep breath and allow a little glimmer of excitement to take its place. This is it. You are going to return to the natural healthy you – conquering the nicotine demon forever. In a few weeks you will look back and wonder how you ever smoked.

Let's get started by exploring how the nicotine demon tricked us into submission in the first place.

Chapter 1

Seeing the Chains

"A cigarette is the perfect type of a perfect pleasure. It is exquisite and it leaves one unsatisfied. What more can one want." Oscar Wilde's 1891 novel, *The Picture of Dorian Gray*

"Let us provide the exquisiteness and hope that they, our consumers, continue to remain unsatisfied. All we would want then is a larger bag to carry the money to the bank." BATCO (British American Tobacco Co) researcher, Colin C. Greig, in a document thought to date from the early 1980s

With an "exquisite pleasure that can never quite satisfy," cigarettes are now as addictive as crack cocaine. Unlike crack however, they are readily available at every corner shop and are completely legal. Also, unlike the crack makers, cigarette manufacturers get to spend 18 billion dollars every year to advertise and market their products worldwide, often covertly and subliminally. That's one hell of a lot of advertising power backing one drug!

In some ways crack addicts have it easy as far as quitting goes. Their lives fall apart very quickly and they either choose to leave their body once and for all, end up in jail, or decide to quit within a relatively short period of time. Cigarettes on the other hand do their damage stealthily so that smokers barely notice their declining health, often until it is too late. You may be aware that you breathe harder at the top of the stairs. You may notice a decreased sex drive, increased anxiety, or a nagging cough. But the real damage is usually found much later, by doctors using X-rays and MRI machines. The "dealers" of the tobacco drug are crafty and want to keep their customers alive and paying for decades. Only then will they pass you over to the medical industry for you to spend any remaining cash you have that hasn't already gone up in smoke.

The Surgeon General estimates that six million people will die prematurely this year (2014) from tobacco related diseases, half a million of whom are in the United States. Can you imagine if any other single thing killed six million people this year? There would be shock and public rallies for an immediate solution to the problem. Not for tobacco deaths though. There's hardly a murmur despite these figures growing year after year. It's like all the war and poverty we see in the world; we've accepted it as something inevitable rather than something completely preventable.

I am so glad that you have decided to take action to reclaim your health and not end up part of this terrible death toll. Perhaps once you are done our next job will be to end the unnecessary suffering of humanity.

Smoking creates negativity on many levels, not just an early death. As smoking becomes more socially unacceptable it creates feelings of guilt, embarrassment, and humiliation. Being a smoker also creates frustration at not being able to stop. It creates fear as you worry about what will happen if you don't stop, or stress as to how you are going to get the next cigarette.

Chemicals in cigarettes themselves also generate negative feelings, such as anxiety and anger, as they wear off. You can feel that anxiety mounting if you don't get the next one on time. You may feel it in your head, neck, chest, stomach, or hands and it feels very real.

All these emotions have a low vibration; they bring you down. Once down you then attract more negative things into your life: health issues, stressful events, and angry people. It's the way the Universe works. Quitting smoking doesn't just improve your health and happiness, but it raises you up, literally changing all aspects of your life for the better.

I'm so glad that you have decided to embark on this journey of increased consciousness and freedom. You are going to enjoy your life far more, once the haze of smoke that surrounds you has finally lifted.

You may not believe quite how different it's going to be, but you'll see!

*****

"None are more hopelessly enslaved than those who falsely believe they are free." Johan Goethe

Twenty-five years ago people may have been honest when saying, "I could quit if I wanted to," but not anymore. Cigarettes have never been more addictive than they are today.

Tobacco has changed a lot since the time when the American Indians puffed on it in their ceremonial pipes or used it for ritual cleansing. In fact the stuff in modern cigarettes bears very little resemblance to this original tobacco at all. Manufacturers have spent a great deal of time and money changing cigarettes to become as addictive as possible and in the process have made them much more deadly.

Genetic Modification

It's estimated that most tobacco now has double the nicotine it used to, due to genetic modification. Kool cigarette maker Brown and Williamson started in 1994, creating a tobacco strain known as Y-1 which had six percent nicotine: twice the normal found in natural cured tobacco.

The chemical engineering used to increase tobacco's addictive quality also allows bacteria genes to be introduced into the genes of the plants as a built-in pest control. These "biochems" destroy the digestive tracts and the reproductive capacity of insects, worms, and beetles, which keeps production high. It does not take much to imagine what in turn it might be doing to us!

To make it worse, since the introduction of genetically modified tobacco, researchers at the Colorado School of Mines in Golden, Colorado, have identified three previously undetected pesticides in cigarette smoke. They are:

Flumetralin: known to be toxic to humans as well as carcinogenic. It is also an endocrine disruptor and is banned in Europe for use on tobacco, but not in the USA.

Pendimethalin: another endocrine disrupter which specifically targets the thyroid. It is also carcinogenic and poisonous to humans.

Trifluralin: also an endocrine disrupter, toxic to humans and carcinogenic, affecting glands and hormones which can lead to breast and prostate cancer.

Despite research proving the dangers of these pesticides all three are approved for use by the EPA[1], who claim *"No information exists for long-term low-level inhalation exposures to these compounds."* It's hard to understand why they don't look a little deeper.

In the United States, most tobacco grown is now genetically modified (as well as most of the corn, sugar beet, cotton, and soy by the way). Modified plants come hand in hand with the toxic weed killer Roundup, which sadly also ends up in tobacco. Oddly enough, nicotine is a great herbicide and pesticide so you think they would use that instead of Roundup. Well, except for the tiny fact that the giant chemical company Monsanto would not make any money.

I met a young man in one of my classes whose uncle had a tobacco farm in South Carolina. Apparently this uncle was given a hefty check and new genetically altered seeds every few years, as well as special chemicals to spray on the crops. They were handsomely paid to use GMO crops rather than natural plants, as these are the "Frankenplants" used to ensure you stay addicted.

Genetic modification is just the tip of the iceberg however, as according to the European Union health website, tobacco additives now account for 10% by weight of cigarettes. Most are put there intentionally. Things like rat poop of course are not!

[1] Environmental Protection Agency in the USA.

Menthol

According to the NCBI Tobacco Control website, from the 1960s onwards cigarette companies particularly targeted women as well as young people and African Americans, by adding more menthol to cigarettes in order to make the smoke feel cooler. Its anesthetizing effect let smokers draw deeper into their lungs while masking the damage that was being done. Little did consumers know but it also had the effect of making the lining of the lung more permeable, or "thinner," so that more nicotine (and tar) could pass into their blood stream, thus making menthol cigarettes more addictive. Smoking a pack of menthols is the equivalent of smoking a pack and a half of normal cigarettes, and no other cigarette will do once you become addicted to the extra menthol. If you are a menthol cigarette smoker you will know exactly what I am talking about.

Alarmingly, a study of more than 500 smokers shows that smokers of menthol cigarettes are twice as likely as non-menthol smokers to suffer strokes and heart attacks. I mean, what woman or African-American person wouldn't love that?

This quote explains a lot: *"Unregulated botanical and chemical additives might have 'multiple use' purposes, such as enhancing flavor and providing for a 'smoother' smoking experience as well as preventing or masking symptoms associated with illnesses induced by smoking. Because inclusion of botanical and chemical additives could reduce, mask, or prevent smokers' awareness of the adverse symptoms caused by smoking (e.g., cough), smokers might continue to smoke even when they are ill, preventing reductions in cigarette consumption and sales revenues"* (Michael Rabinoff, DO, PhD, Nicholas Caskey, PhD, Anthony Rissling, MA, and Candice Park, BS).

Ammonia

In order to ensure even fewer smokers quit and more people got hooked (after all, you have to replace all the dead "cash cows" as well as generate higher premiums for the shareholders), on top of all the other chemicals added to cigarettes[2], ammonia was also added to tobacco.

"The secret of Marlboro is ammonia." Scientist in 1989 Brown & Williamson Tobacco report

"It was noted that Ammonia treatment was now being used increasingly widely. For security reasons, it was suggested that, in future, the treatment should be referred to by a code name." Minutes of the Tobacco Strategy Review Team (BAT) meeting held on September 17, 1990

Many different code names have been used within the tobacco industry to describe the augmented impact of ammonia chemistry, including volatile nicotine, pH effect, amelioration, extractable nicotine, burley impact, and increased satisfaction or augmentation. Channing Robertson, a Stanford chemical engineer, was barred from using the term "freebase nicotine" in his 1998 testimony for the plaintiffs in Minnesota v. Philip Morris, so he testified instead about what he called "crack nicotine." I think it's his description that sums it up best.

Ammonia breaks up nicotine molecules, making them volatile, so more can be absorbed at a faster rate. The same process turns cocaine into crack. Essentially, ammonia allows you to "free-base" nicotine. The fact that tar, poisons, and heavy metals now also pass more easily

[2] The complete list of 599 chemicals is at the end of the book.

into the blood and organs means cigarettes have been able to murder people on a scale outdoing even mass killers like Stalin or Mao. It is estimated that between the two of them they were responsible for one hundred and five million deaths in all – a mere ten percent of deaths caused by smoking cigarettes so far.

Perhaps most alarming is the fact that volatile nicotine can't be detected by the smoke analysis machines that monitor cigarettes for nicotine content. This allows American Spirit cigarettes to market themselves as *natural*, while containing more than three times more volatile nicotine than even Marlboro![3]

Acetaldehyde

The greed of the people that run the tobacco industry is insatiable.

Back in the 1990s Philip Morris persuaded a young scientist called Dr. Victor DeNoble to find alternatives to nicotine that could be added to tobacco. During his research he discovered the opiate-like effect of a chemical called acetaldehyde that forms from sugars when burned. It already existed in tobacco but could be added in larger quantities to reinforce the addiction.

In his experiments DeNoble set out to find out what effect nicotine and other chemicals had on rats. They were connected to an intravenous tube that would give them a dose of whatever it was if they pressed a lever. He discovered that when you addict rats to nicotine they pressed that lever 120 times a day. When offered acetaldehyde, they demanded the drug 240 times a day. However, when nicotine and

---

[3] According to James Pankow of Oregon Health and Science University in Portland, American Sprit produces 36% volatile nicotine while Marlboro generates 9.6%.

acetaldehyde were mixed together that little addicted rat pressed the button 540 times a day. In fact this combination is so potent that some rats stopped eating or sleeping, preferring instead to hit the button until they died. To the delight of the CEO (and no doubt the shareholders), acetaldehyde was immediately added to cigarettes. DeNoble on the other hand was shocked and appalled.

Cigarettes became about 6x more addictive overnight. The Marlboro brand was the first to contain acetaldehyde and it quickly became the world's number one brand. Other brands soon followed suit and despite evidence starting to emerge as to the dangers of smoking, people carried on smoking because it was too hard to stop. Profits soared and no doubt many yachts were bought and much Crystal bubbly was consumed. All the while people like you and me puffed and paid, puffed and sickened, puffed and died.

DeNoble eventually turned against his employer as a whistleblower and testified in Congress about the dangers of smoking. This led to major reforms and record fines against the tobacco industry. Today, he's a nationally known anti-smoking advocate who speaks to 300,000 students a year about what he calls the tobacco industry's "deceptions."

Dr. Jeffrey Wigand was another courageous whistleblower who suffered all kinds of attacks by the industry when he objected to killing people for profit. Like Dr. DeNoble, he had been recruited on the pretext of developing a safer cigarette. A year later, the program was scrapped as "safer" turned out to mean "less profitable." He had proof however that additives were purposely being used, knowing they posed a serious health risk, while the spokesmen for the tobacco companies tacitly lied to the public about it. He was finally spurred to speak out when his bosses and all the other bosses in the industry committed perjury in court saying they did not believe nicotine to be addictive. After having to live for years with armed bodyguards, Dr. Wigand now runs the Smoke-Free Kids organization.

You may wonder why they're not required to mention ammonia or acetaldehyde on the side of the pack. You may question why bed manufacturers are required to put a page of disclosure on every mattress while combustible materials designed to be absorbed by the human body are left completely unchecked?

The answer is money.

Obscene amounts of money – millions of dollars in lobbying and political payouts. Truckloads of cash to pay lawyers to fight anyone advocating full disclosure. Buckets of cash to pay people to intimidate whistleblowers and vast gobs of dough to pay for PR and advertising. Still leaving more dollars to create misleading information: like counting ammonia as being a "natural" tobacco component, even though it's purposefully augmented.

According to *The Tobacco Atlas*, total revenues from the global tobacco industry approach half a trillion U.S. dollars annually. In 2010, the total profit from the six leading companies was $35.1 billion – equal to the combined profits of Coca-Cola, Microsoft, and McDonald's. If Big Tobacco were a country, it would have a higher domestic gross income than countries the size of Poland, Saudi Arabia, Sweden, or Venezuela.

It's not just the tobacco industry riding this gravy train. What about the pharmaceutical industry? It's great news for their sales of course with so many sick and dying needing medical help. They also profit massively from the fact that cigarettes are now so hard to quit. According to a report by Visiongain, UK, the market for pharmaceutical smoking cessation products was already $2.4 billion in 2012. And doctors? Even if they don't like to see their patients suffering personally, financially speaking they rely on it to get paid, particularly the cardiologists and oncologists. We've created an insane situation where the pursuit of money is at the expense of human happiness and well-being.

Governments take their cut too. The federal and state governments in the United States raked in over $24 billion in 2009 from taxation on tobacco, which is more than the tobacco companies made in profit themselves. According to the Surgeon General a smoker is likely to die 10-15 years earlier than a non-smoker so governments also get the additional benefit of having a lot less retirement money to pay out. Cha-ching!

It's not really cha-ching in the long run of course, as the real cost of smoking on society is huge as people become sick and need medical help. According to *The Tobacco Atlas* (Eriksen, Ross and Mackay) during 2000–2004, the value of cigarettes sold just in the United States averaged $71 billion per year, while cigarette smoking was responsible for an estimated $193 billion in annual health-related economic losses. As far as the emotional loss goes, how does one even begin to quantify that?

The logical thing would be to not allow the manipulation of tobacco so that people could break the addiction. The money that's made from smokers is why it hasn't happened. So many people profit, and at the top of the pile are the tobacco manufacturers themselves. All they know is, for every *death* recorded from tobacco use another $6,000 in profit has gone into their coffers.

Keeping you addicted and paying is therefore these psychopaths' chief concern.

My use of the word psychopath may shock you, but the definition of a psychopath is one who is unable to feel love, empathy, and compassion, and therefore experiences no guilt. There is no "right" and "wrong," there is just what works for him or her to get more power and money. They are one hundred percent ego – self-centered and self-serving – and enjoy feeding off the suffering of others. I feel that the people at the top of the tobacco industry pyramid fit this description perfectly.

They've used you to make money. You may have chosen to smoke in the beginning but after that the choice was removed. You were purposely turned into an addict to make them rich.

The fact that smoking results in terrible suffering physically, mentally, and economically for people all over the world means nothing to its creators as long as they get more wealth and power. Their selfish compulsion knows no bounds, and can never be satisfied it seems.

They depend on you, however, to keep feeding their diabolical system.

All of the changes we want to make in the world actually start with the individual. That means it starts with you. You stop smoking. This then inspires some of your friends to stop smoking, then their friends and their friends' friends get inspired to quit too. Pretty soon the cigarette companies have no more money to keep pushing this poison onto our children and it's Game Over. Not participating is the only way to defeat any of the insane corruption and evil we see in the world right now, but let's begin with the tobacco industry.

To help you start the ball rolling I'm going to explain exactly what is being sucked into your lungs from that slim, white, innocent looking cigarette. That wolf in sheep's clothing.

Five-minute contemplation: "The effect of my smoking has been felt across the entire universe."

Just sit for a while and let those words sink in.

Chapter 2

Seven Thousand Chemicals

You shall know the truth and the truth shall make you mad." Aldous Huxley

When you draw on a lit cigarette, the end burns at a staggering 1560F (850C), according to an internal study by British-American Tobacco Co. The combustion causes the tobacco leaves, the bleached paper, and the added ingredients to break down into 7,000 different elements and chemicals. Of these, around 250 are carcinogenic which means they are proven to cause cancer.

A short list would include formaldehyde, used to embalm dead bodies; benzene, used to fuel your car; arsenic, a deadly poison; vinyl chloride, used to make plastic coffin liners; and polonium 210, which is radioactive. According to a government study, the polonium absorbed by smoking a pack a day for a year gives off as much radiation as receiving 200 chest X-rays, which is disturbing to say the least.

Various poisonous gases are also released, such as carbon monoxide, found in car exhaust; hydrogen cyanide, used in chemical weapons;

butane, used as lighter fluid; ammonia, used in cleaning products; and toluene, used in paint thinners.

Toxic heavy metals in tobacco include lead, chromium, and cadmium, which damage the brain and internal organs.

Not surprisingly cheap cigarettes are even more deadly. They are made using recycled paper, which contains dioxin. Dioxin has been listed as "*having no safe dose or threshold below which Dioxin will NOT cause cancer.*" This is NOT good.

If you use smokeless tobacco you might think all this talk about what's in a cigarette does not concern you. Think again. As well as nicotine, tobacco dip contains cadmium, formaldehyde, lead, n-nitrosamines, polonium 210, acetaldehyde, benzopyrene, uranium 235, large amounts of salt, fiberglass, and even sand.

If someone told you to knowingly breathe in or chew on any of these things there is no way you would do it, and you would seriously doubt the sanity of anyone who did.

And what does it say on the pack or the tin about all this?

Nothing.

At the end of the book I will go over a more complete list of all the additives that are purposely added to keep cigarette smokers hooked. They include things you might never think of, like coffee, tea, chocolate, rum, apple juice, maple syrup, sugar, snakeroot oil (which I find appropriate), and oddly, even smoke flavor.

Robert Proctor, author of *Golden Holocaust: Origins of the Cigarette Catastrophe and the Case for Abolition*, talks about additives: "*Just in cocoa shells alone, there are ... millions of pounds of licorice (and) diamonium phosphate, which is a freebasing agent. Chocolate and cocoa are added because they contain the alkaloid theobromine which is a broncho-dilator (*that*)* *basically makes the poison go down easier. And those are just some of the things that are there on purpose. There is also all kinds of stuff in there by accident... if you look at the secret documents, it talks about there being shards of plastic and pesticides and bits of wire and even blood of various sorts."*

Many of these additives are benign when ingested. That is, if you eat them they pass through the digestive tract without disrupting the body, which is how the tobacco companies get permission to use them. But when they are burned, they change into something very different. For example Glycerol turns into acrolein, which is carcinogenic and highly toxic.

It's this kind of information that the tobacco industry goes to great pains to keep from public scrutiny.

In fact they spend a lot of time and money hiding or distorting the truth and creating a fake reality that somehow cigarettes are a normal part of human life.

Five-minute contemplation: "I have the authority to direct my life."

Chapter 3

Nicotine – The Drug

"There is little doubt that if it were not for the nicotine in tobacco smoke, people would be little more inclined to smoke than they are to blow bubbles or to light sparklers." M.A.H. Russell, "The Smoking Habit and Its Classification."

Learning how nicotine works will help you understand the nature of the beast and how to overcome it.

Nicotine is a psychoactive drug similar to cocaine or heroin. It travels to the brain in as little as seven seconds after it has been absorbed into the blood stream.

Nicotine is why you enjoyed smoking stinky, repulsive, anti-social, disease-creating bonfires of dead leaves and chemicals for all those years despite never having had the urge to suck down the smoke from your neighbor's leaf pile.

Every time you have a puff you are medicating yourself. In fact you are altering your brain chemistry about 70,000 times a year if you smoke a pack a day. Not only that but Dr. Simon Ridley, from

Alzheimer's Research UK, says, *"Research has repeatedly linked smoking…to a greater risk of cognitive decline and dementia,"* so you are medicating yourself with something that can eventually make you lose your mind!

Before this happens however, it temporarily enhances alertness. Once nicotine enters your system it raises both the heart and breathing rates because it resembles a chemical found in the brain known as acetylcholine. It's this effect that leads a smoker to believe that cigarettes help them concentrate. If it really did though, we would expect to see companies advertising for high level employees who smoked. For example, "*Pilot Wanted – only two pack a day people should apply.*" You never see that of course, because apart from the increased cost of employing a smoker, nicotine actually has the effect of clouding the mind when it wears off. The longer the smoker is prevented from smoking, the more distracted and agitated they become. Smoking that cigarette is simply a way of briefly clearing the fog created by the previous cigarette, before it re-forms.

How much better to live in the sunshine all the time!

Nicotine also triggers more blood sugar to be released, which gives you a feeling of heightened awareness. This is how you are able to satisfy yourself with coffee and cigarettes when your body tells you that you are hungry. Your cells get no minerals, vitamins, enzymes, proteins, or fats, but are tricked by a turbo charged boost of chemical energy. Rather like whacking a donkey on the backside with a stick instead of feeding it a bucket of oats and carrots!

When you smoked your first few cigarettes you experienced a nice rush of dopamine making you feel a little bit "high." After a few weeks of smoking though, your brain's chemistry began to change. It radically reduced the manufacturing of its own natural dopamine as it made the adjustment to the excess levels created by nicotine. Receptors in your brain actually changed shape to accommodate the foreign nicotine molecules. This then resulted in you *needing* cigarettes in order to maintain healthy levels of dopamine within your brain. Without dopamine, you become miserable and irritable, so you look to another cigarette to relieve those symptoms.

This means once again that the cigarette you smoke now is simply to relieve the negative feelings triggered by the cigarette you had an hour ago. This is the vicious cycle of addiction that you are walking away from.

Hallelujah!

Because of how nicotine works, trying to quit "cold turkey" can be tough, causing all kinds of stressful withdrawal symptoms. Even someone who has smoked for just a few weeks could feel dizziness, depression, digestive problems, anger and impatience, anxiousness, difficulty concentrating, trouble sleeping, headaches, hot flashes, and restlessness. No wonder people pick up another cigarette. Don't worry though: we will shortly discuss strategies for overcoming these withdrawal effects.

*****

We all have stress in our lives and I will be teaching you ways to release stress naturally without having to rely on anesthetizing yourself with a cigarette. The major thing that has been causing stress is not your *life*: it's the cigarettes themselves.

Many smokers believe smoking calms them down and de-stresses them, and you may be one of them, but really it's the other way around. Nicotine actually causes stress. Sorry to burst your bubble on this one!

When you take a puff on a cigarette or cigar, or put chewing tobacco in your cheek, hundreds of neuro-chemicals are released into the brain. One of these is adrenaline.

When adrenaline is triggered, the heart beats faster and the body gets set for a "fight or flight" response. This is a very useful mechanism when a tiger jumps out of the jungle at you, but less so when you are simply relaxing on the couch with no tiger in the vicinity. When the action of fight or flight is not actually required cortisol is released by the brain, which swings the body into a feeling of anxiety. This unpleasant, stressed feeling is again temporarily relieved by another hit of nicotine, and so it goes on.

The problem is, when we get stressed, our survival instinct switches off the intelligence of our human cortex – the conscious part of our brain that knows we longer want to smoke – and the reptilian brain takes over. This reptilian brain or hypothalamus convinces itself there is real danger whenever there is adrenaline in the system. Sadly, it can only suggest what is has done thousands of times before to make the apparent "danger" go away: smoke.

Once you get to a certain point of anxiety you may have found yourself like an automaton reaching for the pack and lighting a cigarette even though you've told yourself categorically that you are not going to do it. It's usually about halfway through the cigarette that the anxiety level drops enough for you to come to your senses and realize the mistake you just made.

Therefore, in order to quit successfully, it's important to stay calm and fully conscious so that the reptilian brain can't accidently sabotage you.

If you have been smoking for a long time you may have noticed that as the years pass, the next cigarette brings you less relief, which makes you smoke even more. In the end, your "fix" will hardly have any effect at all. The irony is that as you get sicker, weaker, and more miserable, the nicotine addict in your head fools you into thinking that cigarettes are your last true pleasure. A cruel, sadistic trick indeed.

You've been trapped like a pet hamster on a wheel, round and round you go, paying at every turn. Squeak! Squeak!

Once you get off that wheel and break out of the cage entirely you will notice how much calmer you feel and how much more easily you can cope with life. Your shame and guilt will be gone and your sense of self-worth will go up. You will also notice how much brighter everything seems and how much happier and more energized you feel.

To make quitting easier, it helps to understand the psychological reasons, as well as the chemical reasons, as to why you might have been smoking.

Five-minute contemplation: "I am no longer part of the artificial matrix of nicotine addiction."

Chapter 4

What Kind of Smoker Are You?

"Do not cure ill with ill and make your pain still heavier than it is."
Sophocles

The nicotine demon keeps you in chains emotionally as well as physically. Our own issues sometimes add to those chains, however. How you smoke can reveal the psychological reason why you keep doing it despite not wanting to, beyond just the chemical addiction to nicotine.

Smoking can be used as a coping mechanism to deal with various issues. When this is the case, it can be much harder to give up. Subconsciously your mind will not want to surrender something it thinks is vital for keeping you functioning, but it will gladly let it go once the issue has been dealt with.

Remarkably, nicotine can act like a stimulant, a relaxant, or an anesthetic. It would be hailed as a miracle drug if not for the disturbing disease and early death side effects. It is very unusual to find a substance that can both speed you up or relax you and even act like a painkiller, but nicotine's mood altering effects can do all three, depending on how you smoke.

So which kind of smoker are you?

A Quick Puffer: You smoke first thing over a cup of coffee. You smoke quickly like it's a job to get done, and you smoke on breaks and as soon as you get off work. You smoke when you feel low or sad, and you tend to smoke between ten and twenty cigarettes a day. Some quick puffers only smoke for part of the day and rarely smoke cigarettes all the way to the end. You think life would be dull and miserable without smoking.

In order to produce a "lifting" effect a Quick Puffer takes short, quick puffs regularly to produce a low level of blood nicotine that stimulates the production of dopamine – which makes you feel happier. If you are someone who takes short puffs to chemically perk yourself up, successful quitting begins with finding ways to add dopamine and stimulation to your life naturally. If you have a job that bores you to death, a relationship that should have ended years ago, or the high point of your day is sitting in front of the TV, perhaps some changes are required in your life. Perhaps it's time to rethink what makes you happy. Perhaps you need a more exciting way to earn a living, or to pursue the painting or writing aspirations you had as a teenager. Perhaps it's time to grow spiritually? It's hard to grow or be anything more than apathetic when your days are spent polluting your body and mind with neurotoxins.

Eating better (organic food, raw food, live food like sprouted beans) and getting your body moving are great ways of increasing your dopamine levels naturally and getting you more energized to move on with your life.[4]

The herb mucuna bean can help raise dopamine levels and St. John's Wort can take the edge off feeling sad.

A Long Puffer: You smoke as soon as you get up and have one last cigarette at night with plenty in-between. You smoke it all the way through and sometimes a couple in one sitting. You see smoking as a break and time for yourself. You smoke before starting a new task and have to have one as soon as your stress levels go up. You believe life is stressful and that smoking calms you down. The idea of quitting makes you feel nervous.

Smokers who want to calm themselves down take longer puffs. This produces high levels of nicotine, creating a mild sedative effect, making you feel calmer. Sadly of course the adrenaline produced at the same time makes you feel nervous again as soon as it wears off.

If you are one of those smokers who draws longer on cigarettes, then it's time to find new ways to de-stress and to take time out for yourself. Breathing deeply is good for this, as is meditation (which can simply be sitting and breathing consciously), yoga, walking, and listening to relaxing music.

Eckhart Tolle, in his book *A New Earth*, tells a story of a Buddhist monk who said we need to meditate 15 minutes a day, and on those

---

[4] On an emotional level, lack of motivation could be caused by grief, apathy, guilt, or humiliation. If this is your case, and you can't shift it yourself, seek help. A Rapid Resolution Therapist, a good Tapping/EFT practitioner, or a hypnotherapist can change your life in as little as one session. If there is no one locally, check out my website www.helenbasinger.com and if it seems right for you we can work together on Skype.

occasions when we have no time to meditate, we should meditate for an hour. The point being that, once you are calm, you will be much more effective and focused for the time remaining. He's saying that time will seem to expand once you are back in that calm space. It's the exact opposite of what happens to you if you smoke. You steal hours from your day to trigger your own anxieties and then spend the rest of the time chasing your tail, thinking about when to take your next cigarette break. Not a lot gets done and the stress increases.

Over time we tend to accumulate stress, and a great way to empty it out is to use the Tapping techniques I describe later in the book. You will then be able to take on a lot more without feeling stressed.

Drinking chamomile or valerian root tea or tincture or rubbing a little lavender oil on your wrists can also help keep you feeling naturally peaceful.

A Deep Puffer: You smoke even before you get out of bed. You smoke each cigarette like it was your last – right down to the butt – and even get up in the night to have another. You have a spare carton in the house and a few packs in the car and sometimes have more than one on the go at the same time. You could be smoking two or even three packs a day. You suffer a lot of physical and/or emotional pain. Quitting cigarettes seems both scary and insane.

Someone who draws deep, hard, and often on a cigarette in order to get an even higher dose of nicotine is stimulating serotonin and opiate activity, producing a strong anesthetizing effect which reduces pain, be it physical or emotional. In fact many people find that physical pain has an emotional root to it.

If you're a Deep Puffer, search out other people who can help you. As well as medical doctors there are chiropractors, deep tissue massage therapists, Tapping or EFT practitioners, hypnotherapists, acupuncturists, trauma therapists, counselors, shiatsu practitioners, energy healers, Reiki masters, spiritual healers, shamans, herbalists, and doctors of Chinese medicine. It doesn't matter what works for you as long as you find something that relieves your pain. Quitting smoking will make up for whatever expenses you might incur, and the important thing is you retake control of your body, mind, and spirit.

Prayer can work miracles too. Ask your Higher-Self, the Universe, Source, or God for help, and be thankful in expectation of your request being fulfilled.

Using cigarettes to medicate yourself is simply masking the symptoms for a brief period of time while setting yourself up for a much worse situation further down the road. It tricks you into thinking it is helping you but really it's just masking the issues, keeping them and you stuck in an endless loop of disharmony. It is not a medication that will ever make you well.

So rise up, take action, do what you need to do to release all your issues so that the nicotine demon can finally be conquered.

Five-minute contemplation: "The consciousness that created the universe dwells within me."

Chapter 5

Tricking Your Subconscious Mind

"To sell a product that kills up to half of all its users requires extraordinary marketing savvy. Tobacco manufacturers are some of the best marketers in the world." Faisal Mahmud

As well as cigarette's sophisticated chemical effect fooling us, cigarette manufacturers have used clever marketing techniques over the years to make breathing toxic chemicals into your lungs seem like a normal, sane thing to do.

"Rather than perceiving smoking to be what it really is, a lethal activity for both the person who engages in it, and for those who are proximal to the smoker, the industry has convinced many that smoking is a natural and normal activity in which we have the right to engage." Jeffrey Wigand and Hope May, "The Right to Choose"

To understand the extent to which we have been manipulated and controlled by tobacco marketing it is helpful to understand the basics of how the mind works.

"The conscious (mind) is essentially nothing more than a computer, while the subconscious is the computer programmer." Dean Koontz, *Night Chills*

The ever-present subconscious mind observes and remembers everything we see, hear, smell, etc. without distinguishing between truth and falsehood. The conscious mind, which starts to develop after birth, acts like a gatekeeper. It takes in very little and filters it through our very limited belief system. Subliminal advertising is designed to get past the gatekeeper without being seen, where it will be acted upon as *fact* by the subconscious mind.

Subliminal advertising has been used since its discovery in the 1950s with the famous advertisements for Coca-Cola and popcorn in cinemas, and is still being used today. Rather than flashing words too quickly for the conscious mind to notice as they did back then, advertisers now use rheostatic control. This plays the subliminal message covertly behind the film using minimal light intensity so that the message is only seen subconsciously. In the same way sound frequency can also be used. There are no actual federal laws against using this technique, which makes you wonder if and how it's being used.

One of the main motivations of our subconscious mind is to alleviate anxiety and protect us. Advertisers know that if they can make your subconscious fearful it will influence your conscious mind to do what it thinks will make things safe again – in this particular case, smoke cigarettes in order to feel safe. You can't get much more ironic than that. This is how they heighten craving in existing smokers in order to get you to smoke more.

For advertisements in print or on billboards a word like "die" can be vaguely printed to make you feel anxious, with the advertisement printed over the top. The word "sex," the outline of a female body, or a phallic shape can be used to make you feel desire. Coca-Cola and various alcoholic drink brands use this sex technique a lot. You don't see it when you look at it unless it's pointed out to you.

An advertising training document from the makers of Kent cigarettes makes it quite clear they are using death and fear to sell cigarettes: "*Since its conception in the early 1960s, the subliminal selling strategy for Kent cigarettes has been based on a variantion of our top-secret Hell-Sell theory. To visually promise the viewer salvation from death, and loss of one's very soul to the devil is an emotional hook that we've cast, over and over again, in varying forms for a variety of clients. Religious beliefs and feelings about death stir deeper emotions than the frequently used sexual strategies.*"

A company using the "sexual strategy" is Camel. In their cigarette advertisements depicting "Joe Camel," the head of the cartoon figure has been alleged to symbolize the "head" of male genitalia. I'll leave that for you to check out yourselves!

Another example of this manipulation of the mind are the countless movies where, after watching a long nail-biting scene of the hero saving the world or as the sexual tension mounts, we are suddenly awash with relief as it all works out and we see someone lighting up a cigarette. You know how this works because you've experienced it yourself many times as you reach for the pause button on the DVR or video so you can go out for a quick smoke.

The makers of Kool and Carlton cigarettes, B&W, had archives that made their way into the public domain that document $500,000 in payments to Sylvester Stallone for promoting their tobacco products in five of his films as far back as the 1980s. According to the Foundation for a Smokefree America[5], the producers of *License to Kill* took a $350,000 payment to have James Bond smoke Lark Cigarettes in his movie. In *Superman II*, woman reporter Lois Lane, a non-smoker in the comics, chain-smoked Marlboros, and the Marlboro brand name appeared around 40 times in the film. Tobacco giant Phillip Morris paid a mere $40,000 to the producers for this. Phillip Morris even managed to place its products in *Who Framed Roger Rabbit* and *The Muppet Movie.* A law called the Master Settlement Agreement now prohibits companies from paying producers to use cigarettes in their films. Despite this, smoking is still portrayed in most top box office movies. According to Reality Check Strikes Again, an organization fighting smoking in Hollywood, eighty percent of all U.S. movies produced and distributed from 1999 through 2003 portrayed smoking: *"In all, Hollywood delivered 32.6 billion tobacco impressions to U.S. moviegoers over five years."* They estimate its influence is enough to replace all the old smokers who die with fresh new teenage ones.

---

[5] Interestingly, according to their website "The Foundation for a Smokefree America was founded in 1989 by Patrick Reynolds, a grandson of the founder of the R.J. Reynolds Tobacco Company. A former pack-a-day smoker, Patrick saw his father, oldest brother and other relatives die from cigarette-induced emphysema, heart disease and cancer. Concerned about the widespread death, disease, and emotional and economic hardship caused by tobacco, Patrick Reynolds divested his RJR stock, quit smoking and became, in the words of former Surgeon General C. Everett Koop, '*one of the nation's most influential advocates of a smokefree America.*'"

What about the shocking quit smoking ads we've been seeing recently in some countries? Given how our minds work, even the graphic labels on cigarette packs designed to get people to stop smoking or the scary advertising campaigns on TV may not be having the effect they were intended to have. Recent research suggests *"that considering death may make some people smoke."* Dr. Gemma Calvert concluded that *"Cigarette warnings – whether they inform smokers they are at risk of contracting emphysema, heart disease or a host of other chronic conditions – in fact stimulated an area of the smoker's brain called the nucleus-accumbens, otherwise known as the 'craving spot.'"*

This is why I seriously debated whether or not to include this next chapter in the book at all. In the end I decided to, BUT if you know you get nervous seeing the lady with the hole in her throat or thinking about the guy with no arms or legs, you'd better skip the next chapter!

If you do decide to read about how smoking harms you, observe how it makes you feel. Pay attention to whether or not your stress level goes up and what that triggers. Once you see how the black magic is done, you're considerably closer to defeating its hold over you.

Five-minute contemplation: "Needing to smoke is no longer a belief I choose to hold."

Chapter 6

Making You Sick

"There are biologically active materials present in cigarette tobacco. These are: a) cancer causing b) cancer promoting c) poisonous d) stimulating, pleasurable, and flavorful." A confidential, 1961 memorandum from the consulting research firm hired by the tobacco company Liggett to do research for the company

Many people have the ability to fool themselves into thinking it could not possibly happen to them. Everyone knows of a grandmother or grandfather who smoked like a chimney and died happily in their bed at the age of 93. And there is a mathematical probability that that *could* be you. Maybe.

And anyway what difference does it make? Don't some people who never smoked get lung cancer? Yes. Only 85% of lung cancer is doled out to smokers, and only seven-eighths of them die within five years. Anything is possible. It's just a matter of whether or not you want to play the odds!

Whatever luck our ancestors had, and however lucky you deem yourself to be, the facts are undeniable. Cigarette smoking is the main preventable cause of death and illness in most countries in the world. In the United States it is responsible for one in every five deaths. The latest figures from *The Tobacco Atlas* show that over 60% of smokers will die from a tobacco-related disease of some kind and almost 50 million people have died worldwide from tobacco just since 2002. For each of those deaths there are twenty people sick and suffering from tobacco-related diseases.

Smoking harms nearly every organ in the body: the heart, blood vessels, lungs, eyes, mouth, reproductive organs, bones, bladder, brain, and digestive organs.

Although most people connect cancer with smoking, tobacco claims most of its victims through heart attacks and strokes. Smokers are six times more likely to have a heart attack than non-smokers: more, if you are overweight. A female smoker having a heart attack is more likely than a male smoker to die on the spot without getting a second chance.

Smoking causes a heart attack or a stroke because of plaque deposits that build up in blood vessels. Plaque is made up of cholesterol, fatty substances, cellular waste products, calcium, and something called fibrin. This sticky plaque builds up in the blood vessels, constricting them. Your blood pressure rises as the same amount of blood is forced through narrower pipes. As more plaque builds up, less and less blood can pass through until the heart eventually cannot keep up. The result is a heart attack.

A stroke occurs when the pressure builds up in the chest or brain to the point where a vessel bursts or gets completely blocked. If it happens in your chest you are killed within minutes. If you manage to survive a stroke in the brain you are likely to end up with speech or mobility issues.

If the plaque build-up is in the limbs or fingers and toes this can lead to tingling, pain, numbness, gangrene, and eventually amputation once the tissue gets so blocked that healing is no longer possible.

About a year ago, someone came to a free group counseling session with me to pick up some nicotine patches because he needed surgery to remove a finger. The doctor quite rightly told him he would not operate unless he quit smoking. The reason the finger was infected to the bone in the first place was that smoking had caused the ends of his digits to become numb. After falling asleep one evening with a lit cigarette in his hand, he had burnt his finger. He continued to smoke so the wound was never able to heal. After a year of much pain in the surrounding finger, the whole thing finally had to be removed. He had cut down on smoking for a while by putting on a couple of patches and told the doctor he had quit so the operation could take place.

If this new surgically inflicted wound does not heal the next joint will have to be removed, and so on. This man is an artist and this is his right hand! Once the surgery was over he immediately went back to smoking the same two packs a day. Such is the hold of the addiction.[6] He passed me on his bike just the other day, puffing away…yelling out something about having cancer now. My heart goes out to him.

[6] It's why it's important to commit to becoming a non-smoker for yourself rather than just quitting for a surgery or to please someone else. If you do it for a short-term reason, the chances are you will go back to it once that reason is over.

If this is making you stressed and feeling like having a cigarette, take a couple of deep breaths to calm yourself down and the craving will lessen.

Smokers' second leading killer is cancer. Smoking damages DNA, which triggers cancer cells to develop. According to the American Lung Association, smoking men are 23 times more likely to get lung cancer than non-smokers, and smoking women 14 times more likely than their non-smoking counterparts. It's not just lung cancer either. Breast, stomach, liver, throat, mouth, skin, and colon are just a few of the body parts affected. According to the World Health Organization smokers are 27 times more likely to get oral cancer. Men who smoke are three times more likely to get cancer of the penis and nine times more likely to get cancer of the anus, while smoking women are three times more likely to get cancer of the cervix.

Keep breathing deeply: the anxiety will lessen in a few moments and you will be back in control.

The third cause of death for smokers is chronic obstructive pulmonary disease. Having COPD makes it hard to breathe, and because the disease is progressive, it gets worse over time. Less airflow means less oxygen, which makes everyday tasks exhausting until even attempting to walk to the bathroom feels like you are suffocating. Many people may have the disease already and not even know it because it develops slowly and the cigarettes themselves are numbing the symptoms.

Many of my clients have it. One as young as 45 told me he could barely walk a block without having to stop and rest. Even though he knew the cigarettes were making it worse, the insidious addiction kept him from seeking help for years. In the end it cost him his job, his home, and almost his life. Thank God he's quit now.

Smoking also causes early menopause, cataracts, gum disease and teeth loss, reduced fertility in both men and women, impotency, and a whole host of other things that reduce your ability to enjoy life, or even continue living it at all.

Like the man who lost his finger, smoking drastically impairs your ability to heal. Osteopaths say the flesh wound made by a broken wrist should heal after two weeks, but that it takes closer to nine with smokers. A bone should normally heal after nine weeks, but for smokers it can take sixteen weeks.

Smoking while pregnant increases the chance of miscarriage and usually results in an underweight baby. It also means the child's brain develops with nicotine in the system, making the child much more likely to smoke in later life.

To top it all off, smoking also gives you stinky breath, skin, and hair, makes being in smoke-free places a withdrawal nightmare, and can force you to huddle outside in the cold with your nicotine addiction. In many places smoking dictates where you live, where you work, and even who you hang out with, taking away your freedom along with your health.

The list of negative things caused by smoking goes on and on but I'll stop here.

Even if you are one of those people who say, *"Well I could just as well get run over by a bus tomorrow"* or *"The whole planet is polluting us anyway,"* just remember that you would not purposely jump in front of a bus anymore than you would lie down by the bus's tail pipe to breathe in the exhaust fumes!

Rather than be fatalistic, decide to be healthy. Be the master of your own destiny. Know that you are co-creating your reality and you can choose to have it any way you want it to be: healthy and free.

When you first started smoking no one showed you the small print as to what the implications were. You really had no idea of the full extent of what you were signing up for. I've just given you the small print, so now you have it.

So? Have I motivated you enough to give you the energy to stand up and quit for good this time? I hope so.

Maybe it's time to rip up that contract to become a nicotine addict that you inadvertently signed all those years ago! Before we do, however, let's take a closer look at who you unknowingly made that contract with.

Five-minute contemplation: "My body is a clean and sparkling temple."

Chapter 7

The Nicotine Demon

"May the devil fly off with your worries. May God bless you forever and ever." Irish saying

Having an addiction that we are struggling to end can definitely feel like we are being controlled by an evil being. We want to quit but "something else" won't let us. The subconscious mind loves images and symbols, so let's give it a visualization that it can respond to in order to rid the "nicotine demon" from your psyche.

Imagine that first pack of cigarettes. Inside is a little nicotine demon. As you puff away for the first time, he jumps unnoticed into your head and settles down comfortably in his new home. He lives off nicotine, and just like a parasite, he needs you, his host, to feed him.

As the years go by, his belly gets fatter and his arms and legs skinnier. He never gets any exercise because you are the one doing all the running around: earning the money for his fix, buying the packs, and taking hours every day smoking the tobacco for him while he sits in your head. His skin gets more wrinkled, his eyes are dull, and his hair is falling out in chunks. His teeth are brown and stained, his eyes are red, and his breath reeks, but he still has a silver tongue.

He's there right now, whispering in your ear, "Today is not the right time, let's do this later, come outside with me, I'm your friend, you love me, life would be awful without me, we have such fun." *He may even be threatening you with dire consequences if you quit. He makes you feel scared.* "People die when they quit you know." *He lies and cajoles. He'll pretty much say and do anything to keep you smoking, so that he can feed.*

I mean, you can hardly blame him! He'll die or have to leave if you stop feeding him.

How does it feel to know he is there in your head: a nasty little parasite; an ugly little demon running your life, ruining your life?

Not so good I suspect! So let's have him taken away.

I want you to imagine that we are now commanding four soldier angels of Light to come down right now (complete with swords and the sound of trumpets!) and throw an impenetrable net of light over this creature. They pull that net really tight around him so he can't move.

Once you have read the next couple of lines you may find it easier to close your eyes as you imagine this whole visualization from start to finish, listen to it on the website www.quitsmokingnowandforever.com, or get someone to read it to you.

See how he reacts to being captured. Is he angry, sad, belligerent, arrogant, or just plain surprised? It does not really matter; his time has come. He was there under false pretenses. You had no idea that you'd let him in or even that he was there.

Game over now though.

Command these soldier angels of Light to take this captured nicotine demon to a place in the Light where he can be retrained to do something positive and useful. After all he must have some uses. He's pretty disciplined – never letting you forget to smoke, or go and buy him a pack at all hours of the day and night.

Ask them also to remove any negative effects that he may have left behind.

Now watch as they take him up in the net, up into the Light, and watch until they disappear.

Now that he's gone, take that contract that you were once fooled into signing and rip it up. It has no authority over you. Really tear it up and throw the whole damned thing in the trash where it belongs!

How does that feel now?

Lighter, now that he's gone? Good to be the victor and know you now run your own life instead of letting this little monster control you? Relieved to be a non-smoker again? Pleased to know you can now be who you were supposed to be from the beginning?

That's great.

Five-minute contemplation: "Smoking belongs to the shadow world."

Chapter 8

Ending the Relationship

Now let's see smoking from another imaginary angle: one where it feels like you have a relationship with cigarettes. Your little friends. You know, the ones where "they have always been there for you, through thick and thin, just you and them taking on the world together." Always with you, appearing to help you get through tough times or making life more fun somehow. Only then to find out they have been emptying your bank account and putting poison in your food.

Have you ever had a relationship that wasn't good for you? Perhaps the person constantly criticized you and lowered your self-esteem. Maybe they stressed you out or made you angry all the time? You split up with them and then got back together, and it was temporarily better but then went back to as bad as you'd ever known it. Do you remember what it felt like when you finally got them out of your system – how much saner you felt, how free, and how your life was more enjoyable in ways you'd forgotten you even enjoyed?

Ending your relationship with nicotine is just the same.

Although it may seem odd to someone who has never smoked, when you've been smoking for a long time it does almost feel like the cigarette has a personality that you relate to.

We've sent the nicotine demon away in the last visualization, so now it's time to break up forever with your toxic lover or friend.

I thought you might enjoy some of these "Dear John" letters to cigarettes, written by some of my clients whilst in the process of extracting themselves from this miserable and unhealthy relationship. I hope it inspires you to write your own farewell letter. It's a very powerful process.

Dear Temptress,

It's still early days and I miss you sometimes but then I come to my senses and realize that us splitting up was the best decision I ever made.

We used to wake up together and drink coffee together but we don't have to do that anymore.

We used to ride together in my truck, but we won't be riding together anymore. It's over.

The truth is you now disgust me. The truth is you were scamming me all along. All you ever cared about was yourself.

Without you I feel better, I can breathe better, my food tastes better, my money stays in my pocket instead of being wasted on you.

On top of this, your pimp Philip Morris is no longer getting rich off me, and that pleases me a lot!

Never ever come back again.

We are done!

Bill

Hi,

We had what I thought was an awesome run for a while.

You were so seductive in the beginning and you made me think I needed you. I was scared at the thought of not being with you. You made me weak and pathetic.

Then recently I suddenly saw you for what you are: a lying, scheming, heartless bitch who only ever wanted me for my money.

It's time for you to go. Get out of my life and take the stinking kids with you.

Bye bye!

Mark

Dear Cigarella,

We walked together for 27 years but now it's time for you to continue alone.

I'm going to be taking a different path from now on: a much nicer one than you have had me walk.

Our relationship is toxic and dangerous for me and it has to end right now.

Good bye. I never intend to see you again.

Lazaro

Dear Marlboro Man,

I thought I loved you these past 42 years but now I realize it was all a cruel trick.

You never cared about ME. You never cared that I was being destroyed. You just wanted me to work for you and feed you. You just wanted a slave and that's exactly what I became. You clouded my mind and slowed down my body. You almost cost me my life!

You need to know that I've taken out a restraining order on you, I've changed the locks on the house and have two Dobermans roaming the yard so don't you ever come back.

And don't think that I'll miss you. I won't. After all what is there to miss? The stink, the wheezing, the waste of money, the feeling of being a prisoner??

Now that I've finally escaped your clutches you will never see me again. I will never let you back!

Good riddance to bad rubbish!

Ayva

PS. And stay away from those children, you creep.

As well as writing a letter like this it can also help to write down what you don't like about smoking, all the reasons you have for quitting, and all the benefits you'll have as a non-smoker. When the going gets tough just reading over these kinds of notes can be very helpful and inspiring.

Five-minute contemplation: "I consciously weave a new belief about me deserving to be a non-smoker."

Just stop and think about this for five minutes. Say it in different ways to extract the full meaning.

Chapter 9

Funeral for a Friend

"Stop all the clocks, cut off the telephone, / Prevent the dog from barking with a juicy bone, / Silence the pianos and with muffled drum / Bring out the coffin, let the mourners come." W. H. Auden, "Funeral Blues"

It's true that even after all we've said about it, somehow cigarettes can still manage to present themselves as our friend. It's time for them to die however so that you can live.

According to Dr. Kübler-Ross, the stages of recovery after a death, which also applies to the loss of smoking itself, are denial, anger, bargaining, depression, and finally acceptance. We need to get you through these stages.

I suspect that as you have got this far into the book you are no longer in denial, but I am sure you remember yourself saying things like *"I could stop if I really wanted to."*

Bargaining with *"just one more"* or *"I'll just get through this stressful period and then I'll quit."* It's easy to lose your cool here. Instead, see it for the lie that it is and move on. Know you will be tested and decide to ignore the voice in your head. Now is the perfect time to quit. Now is all we have. As one of my clients reminded me the other day, "*If not us, then who? If not now, then when?*" a great quote from John E. Lewis.

Imagine it's been a few days since you quit. You expected to feel really pleased but instead you feel miserable and depressed. You think back on your life with your "friend" the cigarette: *"Ah, the good times we had, just you and me."* You contemplate sending a note and flowers, but then you come to your senses and remember that this friend was planning to slowly kill you!

You go out for a walk and appreciate nature and all the good things in your life, you focus on what you want to create from now on, and suddenly the depression lifts.

You keep going, one day at a time, and suddenly it clicks. There is acceptance. In the case of the loss of smoking this moment comes with a clear picture of who this friend really was. You see how you were being manipulated but accept your responsibility in it too. You forgive yourself. You realize how much better it feels to be back to your natural, normal self: loving and caring for yourself and having healthy, loving relationships with real living beings.

If you are reading this and don't relate to thinking of a cigarette as your little friend, you might experience it more like a social prop. You know – something to do while you are waiting for someone, something to do with your hands, something that makes you feel more confident socially. If it were true that it's just a prop, then you could just as well play with a cinnamon stick, a toothpick, or even an unlit cigarette. It would not do the trick of course, as what you are really trying to do is medicate yourself to reduce anxiety.

A substitute prop could help though as long as you combine it with deep, slow breathing to calm you down. Just as if you were taking long puffs on a cigarette but with fresh clean air entering your lungs instead of toxic fumes.

Cinnamon sticks are good because you can suck through them and play with them between your fingers, plus they have a nice flavor. They also help with regulating blood sugar and reducing cholesterol. Natural licorice sticks can also work. Beware of chewing on too many though as licorice raises blood pressure.

Five-minute contemplation: "My desire to quit smoking ripples out into the web of consciousness."

Chapter 10

Craving is an Emotion

Dr. David R. Hawkins created a tool that he calls the Map of Consciousness. In it he ranked emotions on a scale of frequency ranging from very low to very high, with enlightenment at the top and humiliation at the bottom. Craving is an emotion situated on the negative part of the scale in-between fear and anger.

Imagine you have not had a cigarette for a couple of hours. You are an hour overdue for a fix. Your fingers start to tap, your jaw clenches, your chest feels tight, and perhaps pressure starts to build in your head. The voice from your subconscious says, *"You need a cigarette right now or something bad is going to happen."*

But really, what terrifying thing is about to happen? Did you ever hear of anyone's head exploding from a craving? Did they actually stop breathing as a result of a craving? Did they die, or have to be taken away by men in white coats?

No. And that's because NOTHING dangerous is going to happen. The drug is cleverly designed to make you feel like it is. The only thing that's going to happen if you don't smoke is that you are going to rapidly return to your natural, normal self. Not just that but your whole vibration is going to be elevated.

In actuality, cravings – whether they feel more like stress or anger – only last a little while and there are many things we can do to release those feelings quickly.

One way is to distract yourself: clean the car, eat an apple, put on some music, clean out the drawer in the kitchen, or take the dog for a walk. Focus your attention on something else.

Another way is to observe the emotion and breathe. I've underlined this because this is a really important skill. Just take a few deep breaths and observe the emotion of craving; notice how it feels. Where do you feel it in your body? Give it a form. What color is it? Face it head on. Keep observing. Notice how it feels in your body. Is it more like anxiety or more like irritation? Keep observing. Don't judge it as good or bad, just as what *is*. Keep breathing slowly and deeply.

After a few minutes of doing this, lo and behold, whatever it was that you were feeling will suddenly lose all its power and evaporate. We are led to believe that we ARE our emotions and we have no control of them. In fact the reverse is true. We can become masters of our emotions. We can change them from negative to positive quite easily and so set ourselves free.

Try it now. Imagine you are having a craving. Observe the sensations you are experiencing as a scientist would observe a Petri dish of bacteria. *"Hum, fascinating…it feels like a black belt squeezing my stomach or a red angry fire in my brain"*…keep observing, with no judgment. Keep noticing what it feels like and…suddenly it's not there anymore. It was all just a clever illusion. My thanks to Eckhart Tolle and his book *The New Earth* for teaching me this.

Go ahead. Try it. You'll be surprised. Close your eyes and feel what a craving feels like. Breathe, and watch it impartially..........and notice how in a few minutes it fades into nothing.

Five-minute contemplation: "I raise myself far above the vibration of fear, anxiety, and anger."

Chapter 11

So Many Benefits to Quitting

"You can't separate peace from freedom because no one can be at peace unless he has freedom." Malcolm X

Your body will start to recover as soon as you quit breathing in these toxic fumes. It's amazing.

To speed up the process of returning to health, visualize these changes happening in your body as you read them. Imagine what should take days or weeks will take minutes, and what should take months or years will take mere hours. Know that you have the power to heal yourself.

Within twenty minutes of your last cigarette your blood pressure drops to a normal level. When you don't have another one it stays normal.[7]

---

[7] This means if you are taking blood pressure medication you should have a checkup shortly after quitting because your need for blood pressure drugs will rapidly decrease once you stop smoking. The same applies to blood sugar. If you are taking medication for type 2 diabetes your need for it will probably go down as soon as you quit because sugar will no longer be released all day long by the nicotine.

Within eight hours of not smoking, the carbon monoxide in your blood has been cleaned out and consequently oxygen levels have returned to normal. You have more energy. As cells are properly oxygenated you become less of a target for cancer. You also no longer have to worry about other people being able to smell the smoke on you.

After forty-eight hours nerve endings start to re-grow in your fingers and toes and skin. You may feel them tingling as they come back to life.

You can start to smell and taste things with the same appreciation of non-smokers, which is wonderful aside from being able to smell other smokers. I'm serious! A whole new world of taste and aroma appreciation opens up within days of quitting – that same world you left when you first started smoking.

Between weeks two and twelve, circulation and breathing improve and it becomes easier to exercise. Natural dopamine production starts again and you start to feel happier. The gray fog starts to lift!

After a month, coughing and sinus congestion and shortness of breath all decrease, energy increases, and the lungs regain their ability to self-clean and reduce infection. Your immune function improves as it's no longer being compromised by toxins.

After twelve months your risk of a heart attack is reduced to half that of a smoker.

After five years your risk of a stroke is that of a non-smoker, and your risk of cancer of the mouth, throat, and esophagus is half that of a smoker.

By ten years your life expectancy is comparable to a non-smoker, and that is a very good place to be.

By fifteen years of being a non-smoker your chance of a heart attack is the same as a non-smoker, and the fact that you ever smoked seems almost surreal.

These are just the main physical health benefits, but there are many others.

Your stress levels will fall dramatically. The endless loop of creating adrenaline and triggering of stress will stop.

You'll look much younger as your skin texture and color improves enormously!

Your choice of friends, partners, and places to live will increase.

You will become more employable. According to studies at Columbus University it costs an employer an average of $5,616 more to employ a smoker rather than a non-smoker due to lost time and increased insurance premiums. As an employer you know who you'd choose!

Plane travel over long distances will become a breeze, and you'll feel pity for the poor smokers on display in the tar stained glass-walled cells in airports.

Think of all of the time you'll save too. Say you smoke twenty a day and it takes five minutes to smoke one. That's an hour and forty minutes. Now add on all the time you spend going to the store, thinking about having one, cleaning up after them, and worrying about not having enough, how to get out of various places so that you can have one, or even thinking about how you really should quit. It's close to two hours every day! For some it's even longer. That's *your* time that could go to learning something new, catching up with friends, bettering the community, being more effective at work, or raising your vibration further with spiritual teaching or music. Very soon you will be taking your time and your life back. It's exciting!

Once smoke-free you have more money to spend on other things. According to the Campaign for Tobacco-Free Kids the average price for a pack of cigarettes in the United States is now $5.58, although in Missouri a pack only costs $3.93 while in five boroughs of New York a pack can cost anywhere from $11 to $13. The average smoker burns through 13 to 16 cigarettes a day, so an average smoker hands over $1,500 a year, while in New York City, it's closer to $3,300. That's having a vacation or not for many people. For others it's an upgrade to the honeymoon suite with champagne rather than a motel with a six-pack in the fridge. Sit down right now and calculate how much you will be saving every year.

You'll stop being toxic to children, animals, and loved ones who come in contact with your second or even third hand smoke – the dust that remains on and around you after a cigarette.

You'll stop feeling like a second-class citizen, hanging out by the trash cans at the back of the building or on the balcony while everyone else is inside or getting promoted in your place of work.

You'll get to stop supporting a very dark and sinister industry.

MOST IMPORTANTLY OF ALL, YOU'LL GET YOUR LIFE BACK. *YOU* WILL RUN YOUR LIFE RATHER THAN THE DEMON RUNNING YOU!

Five-minute contemplation: "I respond to the vibration of perfect health."

Chapter 12

Becoming a Non-Smoker

Do you remember the calm and quiet that resided inside your head before nicotine took control?

Do you remember the sense of well-being you felt before you took that first cigarette and the nicotine rewired your brain?

Do you remember what it was like not having to smoke?

It was good, right?

It's been so long you can't remember? It's okay. Imagine what it might have been like. It was good, believe me. Allow yourself to know what it feels like.

Are you ready to return home to the "real" you, permanently?

Excellent. Let's go.

Take a moment to do this little visualization. Read it through first and then close your eyes and run it through in your mind or have someone else read it to you. You can also find it on the website www.quitsmokingnowandforever.com.

Go back to a few months before you ever started smoking. See what you are wearing, how you wear your hair. See how young you are, how fresh your breath is, how bright your skin is, how shiny your eyes are, how clear your mind is. See how innocent you are. See how naïve you are about cigarettes.

Now go back as yourself, as you are now, and go up to this younger you and explain everything you now know about smoking. Explain about the "evil empire" of the tobacco industry. Explain that cigarettes are not what they seem. They are not cool or fun or sexy. It's all a carefully crafted illusion. They are full of corruption, greed, and harmful intent. They destroy your body, cloud your mind, make you fearful, and keep you operating at less than your full potential.

Tell this younger, innocent you how bright they are and how proud you are of them. Tell them they are too clever to be fooled by this sneaky trick that will cost years of their life and vast amounts of money. Tell them how smoking has made you short of breath and low in energy. Tell them it's killing you slowly and you want it to be different for them. Tell them to remember everything you have told them.

Now have that younger you go forward to that moment when they first had a cigarette. If you can't remember exactly when it was, you can imagine the kind of circumstance it may have been.

Imagine you are there and now see the new scene unfold: cigarettes are there, you are about to light one but suddenly you remember all the things you have been told by the older you. You withdraw your hand and decide not to do it. It's not for you. You are not fooled by this trick to turn you into a slave. You see it for what it really is: a con. The others can do it if they like but you are going to stay free and alive!

Feel proud that you made the right decision.

Now run through your life from then on, up to the present, imagining cigarettes are out of the equation. See the parties and social events with you smiling and happy, being around smokers or non-smokers and having no desire to smoke even if they do. See yourself having no reason to smoke. See yourself in all those moments of reflection, of relaxation, just sitting and breathing cool fresh air, appreciating all the things around you and all the good things in your life. See yourself at work, more efficient, calmer, more energized, happier. See yourself looking younger and brighter, more confident, less guilt ridden. Appreciate how good it feels to have that life. See how everyone around you is so much happier too.

Imagine there is a you in a parallel Universe just like this, who grew up never to smoke. See them there and jump now into this new life. Step over. Become that new person. Leave the smoker-you behind.

That's great. You have just told your subconscious mind that you choose to be someone else, someone who never smoked. Allow yourself to be a non-smoker.

Allow yourself to choose this new path and to never look back. Never ever doubt your decision to break free

And so it shall be.

And to make sure let's create a plan.

Five-minute contemplation: "Everything exists for me as a possibility."

Chapter 13

The Plan

"Man is free at the moment he wishes to be." Voltaire

So now you know what you are up against. A tobacco industry that has spent billions of dollars creating a drug that is as addictive as crack, in order that you pay them thousands of dollars, year after year, while slowly killing yourself. It's time to put together a strategy to get you out of this bind. Of course part of the plan is already happening – you are already moving away from that smoker that you were. You already feel different.

The funny thing is, if you believed, really knew in your heart, that you were free right now, knew you were perfect, in perfect balance and health, in need of nothing, you would be!

On the one hand, everything I've said up to this point is true about the chemicals, the brain, and the addiction. However, on a metaphysical level it's all a mirage. You are free from cigarettes, right now.

You could just decide that you are a non-smoker and so it would be. Just walk away and leave it behind.

In fact, let's see where you are with this. Put the book down for a few hours and see for yourself how easy it is to keep from smoking.

Sometimes this is easier said than done because we lack faith. We are brought up to only believe in what we perceive with our physical senses. We are products of a material world, not realizing that we are masters of the universe!

So, if you need proof, we will go through the tried and tested process of quitting. We will satisfy your mind by allowing the process to slow down and use all kinds of physical tools and actions, so that you can finally know that you are a non-smoker.

Basically you need something to make the physical withdrawal symptoms less severe so that you can hold firm. Going "cold turkey" is difficult because the feeling of anxiety can become overwhelming as the reptilian brain's "fight or flight" mechanism kicks in, screaming for you to smoke. This stress mechanism cuts off the connection to the intelligence of your cortex or human brain so you literally forget everything you are supposed to do, or not do. Fear also disconnects you from your intuition or your heart-intelligence, and it's your heart that would tell you to be free and live your life in health and happiness.

So, to prevent the chemical reaction which causes this unhelpful disconnection and anxiety, there are a number of things to do. The first would be to do the Tapping session on 'Fear of Quitting.' You can find it on the website at www.quitsmokingnowandforever.com.

If you want to go straight for a physical aid you can use various herbs, homeopathy, foods, or nicotine replacement therapy (NRT). It would be a good idea to read about all the alternatives before making your decision as to which is going to work best for you.

Five-minute contemplation: "There is no limit to what I can be."

Chapter 14

Seventeen Herbs to Help With Quitting

"Everything on earth has a purpose, every disease an herb to cure it." Mourning Dove, Christine Quintasket (1888-1936)

Plants have been used for medicinal purposes long before recorded history. In fact it was the mainstay of medicine right up until the dawn of the pharmaceutical industry less than a century ago.

With all the unwanted so-called "side effects" as well as the cost of modern drugs, many people now prefer to treat themselves with herbs. They come in the form of dried roots, stems, leaves, flowers, or seeds in herbal teas, capsules, tinctures, or essences.

There are many herbs that can help you become a non-smoker. Some calm you down while others cheer you up. Some help you sleep and some can act as a stimulant, while yet others help you detoxify your body.

Some, like mint found in candy, gum, or tea, can even be used as an alternative ritual to smoking.

In describing the following herbs, I will sometimes mention potential side effects or drug interactions. If you are on any medication please consult a physician before introducing *any* herbs or supplements to your diet.

Lobelia/Indian Tobacco

The herb lobelia or "Indian Tobacco" despite its name is not tobacco. It does have a very similar molecular structure however. Once in the brain it satisfies the nicotine receptor sites and releases dopamine and blood sugar, making you feel like you've just had a cigarette. It's very effective. It also tastes pretty bad, just like a cigarette.

It is fast acting, natural, non-addictive, and safe when used in small doses. In higher doses you get a clear understanding of why one of its other names is puke weed! Like all herbs, it is supposed to be taken in the correct dosage and when overdone can be dangerous.

The herb can be purchased either as capsules or as a tincture. A tincture is made in an alcohol base to dissolve it. Lobelia is sold for asthma and bronchitis and helps heal the lungs, **but don't follow the instructions on the bottle** (which tells you to put ten drops in water and drink it or swallow a capsule). We want it for its ability to mimic nicotine and to do this we need just a tiny amount, absorbed through the lining of the mouth.

You should apply one drop or 1/5 of the powder from one capsule inside your cheek every 1-2 hours. It is often easier to put the drop on your finger and then rub it on the inside of your mouth. The best way to use the powder is to empty the capsules into a small bag and then use a pinch at a time once you know what 1/5 of a capsule of the powder looks like. I found out about it from an excellent book by James Hamilton called *Quit Smoking in Four Days*. He quit a heavy habit using lobelia alone.

This is the link to his website: http://www.quit-smoking-in-four-days.net/

You could simply follow his method and I believe you could be successful but with one caveat. As he describes in the book, during those four days he went through some extreme emotional reactions like anger and depression. A few days did not give him the time people sometimes need to process the emerging emotions and to practice being non-smokers. Nor did he have the opportunity to learn techniques for dealing with negative emotions, instead of the usual anesthetizing of them with nicotine. Despite conquering the physical urge to smoke, such overwhelming negative emotions could push you back into nicotine's arms, which is why it is important to learn and use the breathing techniques and Tapping that I teach you in this book as well as use the lobelia.

An additional benefit of lobelia is that it releases fat just like nicotine does and suppresses appetite, helping you to not gain weight. Also, according to Michael R. Peluso, PhD, *"The primary active ingredient in the plant does hold some promise for the treatment of drug addiction,"* and it could also lessen the desire for alcohol. There are strangely very few human trials of lobelia in any context, but after seeing many of my clients use it very successfully to stop smoking (and not put on weight) I am a firm believer in its efficacy. If your local health food store does not stock it you can find it on my website.

Mucuna Pruriens

As you now know, smoking cigarettes lowers your body's own production of dopamine, making you feel sad if you don't get the nicotine-induced version. Mucuna pruriens or "Velvet Bean" is a wonderful plant that kills cravings by increasing dopamine. It's a mood enhancer that makes you feel happy. As well as L-dopamine it also contains small amounts of serotonin, DMT, and even a tiny bit of nicotine, which could also help wean you off the cigarette.

Mucuna pruriens also causes cortisol levels to go down, making you feel calmer.

It regenerates the lungs, improves the immune system, reduces body fat and cellulite, and increases bone density.

For all you men out there, you may be interested to know it increases testosterone and improves fertility too (unlike cigarettes which do quite the opposite!).

It can cause lucid dreams but usually helps you sleep better and wake up more rested.

It should not be used if you are taking pharmaceutical MAO inhibitors.

The "Secrets of Longevity in Humans" website provides an interesting discussion of mucuna pruriens – I recommend checking it out.

*****

While lobelia and mucuna pruriens are the herbs I recommend the most, there are a plethora of other natural herbs that may assist you in quitting, depending on the obstacles you encounter on the way.

Oat straw or **green oats** can be used as a remedy for anxiety and craving. According to 2011 research published in the *Journal of Alternative and Complementary Medicine, "The herb (oat straw) has recently been proven to aid in cognitive performance in the brain,"* so helps with that fuzzy brain feeling. You can buy it as a tea or a tincture, as you can the following herbs.

Coltsfoot, horehound, and mullein help eliminate tar and other foreign substances from the lungs.

Mimosa relieves the headaches and anxiety most smokers experience when quitting.

Passion Flower promotes calmness and relaxation, which will help with the irritability you may experience.

Peppermint leaf has relaxation and detoxification powers.

Ginger root aids in digestion and relieves the nausea that nicotine withdrawal sometimes produces. You can make a tea from the fresh root.

Ginseng has been shown to prevent nicotine-induced release of the neurotransmitter dopamine. Ginseng is usually bought in capsule form.

St. John's Wort can be bought as capsules and is used primarily and very effectively for depression. There is some research that shows it can help people quit smoking.[8]

Skullcap can be used in the treatment of anxiety and nervous tension.

Eleuthero Root combats stress and fatigue and helps boost the immune system.

Elderberry Flower protects against inflammation of the upper respiratory tract.

---

8 According to the book *Natural Cures for Common Conditions* by Stacey Chillemi and Dr. Michael Chillemi D.C., although St. John's Wort is safe when taken alone, it can interfere with the effectiveness of prescription and over-the-counter drugs, such as antidepressants, drugs to treat HIV infections and AIDs, drugs to prevent organ rejection for transplant patients, and oral contraceptives. St. John's Wort is not recommended for pregnant or nursing women, children, or people with bipolar disorder, liver disease, or kidney disease. You should not take it for a few months after having surgery with general anesthetic.

Echinacea Purpurea helps stimulate the body's resistance to infection, disease, fever, and blood poisoning.

Safflower contains anti-tumor properties.

As you go through the process of becoming a non-smoker, become aware of how you feel physically and mentally and use the herbs that are going to best ease that particular issue. Taking advice from a qualified herbalist will always get you the best results.

You might balk at the additional cost of these herbs, but when compared to the real cost of smoking they are worth every penny. Remember that to win this battle you have to be prepared to do whatever it takes.

Again, if you are taking any prescription medication it would be advisable to check with your doctor before taking any herbs. Herbs are medicine.

Five-minute contemplation: "I choose to think that quitting smoking is easy."

Chapter 15

Ten Homeopathic Remedies

"There have been two great revelations in my life: the first was bebop, the second was homeopathy." Dizzy Gillespie

Homeopathy uses the energy patterns of plants and minerals to heal similar living energy patterns that are diseased. For example the remedy coffea, derived from coffee beans, is used to relieve insomnia and hyperactivity or in helping to kick an addiction to coffee.

Homeopathic remedies are created by diluting a substance in distilled water until only the energy signature or memory remains. Higher dilution produces a stronger remedy. You buy them as tiny white pills that you put under your tongue until they dissolve. Boiron USA's website is a great place to purchase them. There are absolutely no negative side effects as we are using energy rather than chemicals to heal the body.

There are a number of homeopathic remedies for smoking and addiction.

Tabaccum, extracted from the tobacco plant, can help with cravings.

Nux vomica is derived from a plant that contains strychnine, a neurotransmitter that causes obsessive compulsive behavior. It is a very effective first step in treating the withdrawal symptoms from quitting smoking.

Lobelia in homeopathic form also helps release addictive energies.

Carbo vegetablis is derived from the charcoal and ash of birch-wood. It revitalizes the state of inertia felt when quitting, while helping you maintain a sense of calm and focus. It also has an affinity with the treatment of heart and lung disease.

Staphasagria is used to treat the suppressed emotions that often lie behind an addiction to smoking. If you are someone who appears rather cold and uptight from the outside and suffers from a history of abuse, humiliation, and/or neglect, this remedy is for you.

St. John's Wort can be used homeopathically for depression and anxiety.

Abies nigra, aconite, and veratrum album are used to relieve the physical symptoms of withdrawal such as nervousness, jitters, increased appetite, and insomnia.

Avena and plantago, extracts of oat and plantain plants, are cleansing extracts that can clear out the nicotine toxin more quickly from your body. These are particularly effective options if you decide to go the all-natural route rather than using nicotine patches (which will be discussed further in Chapter 17).

There is a combined homeopathic remedy called **Stop It Smoking**. It contains caladium seguinum, avena sativa, euphorium officinarum, ignata amara, lobelia inflate, nux vomica, and pasiflora incarnate.

Though homeopathic remedies can be purchased over the counter it would be wise to seek the assistance of a trained homeopath when deciding on how to treat addiction or chronic mental, emotional, or physical illness.

Homeopathic remedies can lose their potency if exposed to strong scents or to radiation, so while using them stay away from coffee, mint, bergamot, menthol, camphor, tea tree, and eucalyptus as they can cancel the delicate vibrational effects of the medicine. Also, don't store them near your microwave or cell phone as the electromagnetic field from them also interferes with homeopathic medicine.[9]

Flower Essences to Soothe You

Bach Rescue Remedy is a combination of flower essences that can be used to calm you down in times of stress and anxiety. A few sprays or drops can help keep your spirits up and your stress down during the quitting process.

Smoke Stop, made by Shaman's Potions, is "a flower essence formula especially formulated to help you through the trying moments when you choose to stop smoking. This formula contains essences to help with irritability, changing habits, agitation, grief and many of the other symptoms that often accompany quitting smoking."

Five-minute contemplation: "Everything I need is always right here."

---

[9] Because EMF energy negatively affects us too, you might like to try putting **orgonite** around your house and office, which transforms it into positive healthy energy. It's made by combining crystals and metals under pressure in resin. You can find out more about it and even how to make it yourself at www.orgonite.com and www.orgonizeafrica.com. It's amazing stuff.

Chapter 16

Vitamins and Foods to Make Quitting Easy

"Oh vitamin B, how I've missed you, / My body has long been bereft / Of your strange but miraculous power / To keep a man healthy and blessed." John Carter Brown, "Vitamin B"

Seven seconds after entering the brain, nicotine causes the release of dopamine but also destroys the vitamins and minerals necessary to maintain it at a normal level. This causes the dopamine to disappear almost as fast as it came, leaving you wanting another cigarette. It also means smoking tobacco depletes the body of many essential vitamins, particularly vitamins B and C.

In order to restore your brain back to its natural state where it makes its own dopamine, introducing several key vitamins, minerals, and amino acids can really help. These are the supplements that seem to be the most beneficial:

Vitamin C

Vitamin B: thiamine, riboflavin, niacin, B6, and B12

Potassium

Magnesium

GABA

L-Theanine and L-Tyrosine

Foods to help you quit

Oats: Soak one tablespoon of ground oats (not oatmeal) in two cups of boiling water over night and drink some before meals. It reduces cravings for nicotine.

Tomatoes: Tobacco and tomato are both members of the nightshade family. Tomato juice and tomato sauce reduce the appeal of cigarettes and help prevent lung cancer.

High Alkaline Foods: These keep the nicotine circulating so you need less to feel okay. Beet greens, dandelion greens, raisins, figs, spinach, quinoa, whole grains, brown rice, almonds, squash, corn, and melon are all good examples of alkaline foods.

Water: H2O has a calming, curative, and detoxifying effect. Keep a bottle of filtered water with you at all times and shower, soak in the tub, swim the sea, soak your feet.

Bananas: B6, B12, potassium, and magnesium in bananas help the body recuperate from the symptoms of withdrawal. Bananas also contain tryptophan, which helps the body make serotonin – which is a mood elevator.

Apples: Eating apples improves lung function. They contain antioxidants that strengthen lung capacity and lower the incidence of coughing and breathlessness.

Oranges: If you are quitting without nicotine patches, oranges can lower the craving by eliminating nicotine from your system very quickly. A glass of orange juice with ½ teaspoon cream of tartar works best.

Five-minute contemplation: "I vibrate with good."

Chapter 17

Nicotine Replacement Therapy (NRT)

"Nicotine patches are great. Stick one over each eye and you can't find your cigarettes." Author unknown

Nicotine patches, puffers, gum, or lozenges, otherwise known as Nicotine Replacement Therapy or NRT, can be used to replace the nicotine in the cigarette so that you can get out of the habit of smoking while still getting a certain amount of nicotine. NRT can also assist those who are trying to give up cigars or chewing tobacco.

Nicotine gum is different than normal gum in that you just chew it briefly and then park it in your cheek so that the nicotine gets absorbed into your cheek lining rather than being swallowed with saliva into your stomach. If you use it the wrong way it makes you feel quite nauseous and doesn't have the desired effect. Nicotine lozenges are parked in the same way but can have a detrimental effect on your teeth if you use them for any length of time.

The inhalers or puffers give you an instant dose of nicotine in a big rush just like a cigarette and can therefore also be really hard to stop once you start. They also don't help you get out of the "hand to mouth," "drawing into your throat," and "sucking into your lungs" habits.

The patch is my preferred nicotine replacement therapy as it does not provide the same addictive spikes of dopamine and adrenaline that the puffers, gum, and lozenges do. I have met countless people who have successfully used these oral products, but years later are still addicted to the puffers, gum, or lozenge! Of course it's better than smoking, but why be addicted at all? Why continue to pay for something that does nothing but relieve the withdrawal symptoms from the previous dose?

The same can be said for e-cigarettes. They might be a healthier option but why be addicted to anything? Why keep paying to have the nicotine demon feed? I'll talk more about e-cigarettes in Chapter 19, but for now just know that they are a very poor tobacco cessation aid.

If you do decide to use these oral products, perhaps because you were successful with them in the past, use them in conjunction with a patch – this method is known as combined NRT. Although combining patches with other nicotine replacement products has been proven safe in scientific studies, I suggest you seek your doctor's approval before embarking on combined NRT. As the NRT regimen progresses, ensure you get off the oral products *before* weaning yourself from the patch. The patch gives you a steady, low, constant dose and is less addictive because of it. It works because it gives you a base of nicotine, prevents you from going deep into withdrawal so that you can stop the smoking habit. They come in 21mg, 14mg, and 7mg sizes.

The best way to use the patch is to wear it 24 hours a day and just see how much you can cut down. If after a week or so you are unable to stop smoking completely, add some more tools. Add the herbs or homeopathy that seem right for you, if you have not done so already. Try the gum or even additional patches if you were smoking more than a pack a day – until you can quit. Then cut any oral NRT products down to nothing *before* you use a lower dose of patch.

How to get the right dose

In my experience most people need to have about half the amount of nicotine from the patch that they would normally get from smoking in a day. One cigarette contains about 2mg of available nicotine, a menthol cigarette delivers about 3mg, and a clove cigarette has about 5mg. Cigars can contain far more, as much as 200mg – but of course not so many are smoked.

So, if you smoke a pack of regular cigarettes per day start with a 21mg patch. If you smoke a pack of menthol go for a 21mg plus a 7mg or 14mg patch.

If you smoke two packs or more then you may need to use two patches if your doctor agrees to it. Add the second one later in the day if you still have strong cravings. In my groups choosing to go the NRT route, I usually start people off on one patch and see how much they can cut down in the first week before adding more. Once the decision has been made to really quit, sometimes a surprisingly low dose of nicotine will be all that is required. I've had people who smoked three packs a day quit on one patch just as I've had pack-a-day smokers who could only quit once they had two patches to completely replace *all* the nicotine they were accustomed to using.

Find the dose that's right for you but don't go crazy. Don't forget nicotine is a poison and excess can cause nausea, sweating, and increased blood pressure and heart rate.

Important things to know when using the patch

Nicotine is an alkaloid and things like coffee, orange juice, alcohol, sugar, artificial sweeteners, and carbonated soft drinks are extremely acidic so when you consume them while using the patch, the nicotine will be neutralized, and you will go into withdrawal. In other words acidic foods and drink stop the patch from working effectively.

Acidic foods include processed foods containing sugar or corn syrup, diet foods containing aspartame (or AminoSweet as they now call it), cow's milk (although alkaline to start with, the process of digestion makes it acidic, unlike goat's milk that stays alkaline), oranges, and beef.[10]

Highly acidic drinks include carbonated beverages, orange juice, alcohol, and coffee. Therefore, during the quitting process it's best to replace coffee with green tea. Cut out sugary foods. Replace sodas and fizzy drinks, such as orange juice and alcohol, with lemon or lime water (which becomes super alkaline in your body), coconut water, or just filtered water. If you can't cut out all these acidic foods and beverages completely, cut down as much as you can. You will notice once you quit smoking that your desire for them drops away in any case, as of course the neutralizing process works both ways. If you smoke you feel the need for more coffee, sodas, or alcohol and vice versa.

---

[10] Note that the human body is supposed to be alkaline for optimal health, with pH 7.3. Otto Warburg won the Nobel Prize for showing that cancer survives in anaerobic (without oxygen) or acidic conditions. Research by Keith Brewer, PhD and H.E. Sataroi has shown that raising the pH or oxygen content in cells to a pH 8.0 creates a deadly environment for cancer. Given the damage you have already done to your body with years of smoking and the well-known health issues resulting from smoking, it would be wise to cut out acidic foods in any case.

Another important bit of information about using the patch is that it can sometimes prevent you from sleeping properly, as of course you don't usually smoke all night long and it can be rather disturbing to your sleep. The reason for keeping the patch on for 24 hours however is so that when you wake up in the morning you are not in withdrawal. The first few days will be the most difficult so I recommend using chamomile, valerian tea, melatonin, or tryptophan (if you can buy it) before bed, to help you sleep.

Nicotine patches often cause very vivid or lucid dreams that can make you think you are not sleeping well. Most people love them but the intensity of these dreams can be disturbing if you are not expecting them. Some would say that this is your emotional issues getting resolved and is therefore a good thing.

If you really struggle with getting enough sleep while using the patch try pulling the patch up and cutting half of it off before bed. If that still does not work take it off, but just know that you may have a strong craving first thing in the morning. Make sure there are no cigarettes nearby and use a drop of the lobelia (discussed in the earlier chapter on herbs) first thing in the morning to immediately fill the gap before a new patch starts to work.

You need to eat something when you put the new patch on in the morning, or you could feel some nausea. It is important to get your blood sugar up with real food, as you are no longer relying on cigarettes to release blood sugar for you.

If you are using more than one patch it works to put one on in the morning and then add another at lunchtime or later in the afternoon. Keep track of which is which so that you replace the right one the next morning.

Don't put a patch on the same place two days running. It can irritate the skin and prevent proper absorption. You can put the patch on your upper arm, upper back, or shoulder. Don't panic if the patches leave marks: they will eventually disappear.

To ensure the patch sticks you might like to rub the area with alcohol and then rinse with water. When your skin is completely dry, stick on the patch, squeezing out any air bubbles and pressing down the edges. Hold your hand over it for about ten seconds until it's completely sealed onto your skin. Warming the skin with a hairdryer beforehand also helps.

It's important the patch sticks really well. If you are very hairy, shave a few spaces on your upper arm and shoulder that you can use. If you sweat a lot during the day you can stick the patch on the top of your foot under socks and shoes. If you still have trouble with sticking, use surgical tape or a waterproof band-aid. After all, if it falls off it's not going to do its job.

As it says on the box, nicotine patches are not advised for people who are pregnant or just recovering from a heart attack, unless under the supervision of a doctor. Of course smoking is even worse!

NicoDerm seems to be the most popular but store brands are cheaper. Sometimes you can get some free samples from quit smoking counseling meetings or phone/online smoking cessation programs.

Nicotine replacement chews

If you are a dipper there are many kinds of herbal chew that can be used to replace the tobacco. They are made of natural ingredients such as tea, mint, wintergreen, etc. Some of the main brand names include Golden Eagle Herbal Chew, Smokey Mountain Herbal Chew, Young's

Herbal Chew, and Bacc Off. "Kill the Can" is a great web resource for more information on these.

Five-minute contemplation: "The universe has designed and wired me for success."

Chapter 18

Pharmaceutical Smoking Cessation Aids

"Death by medicine is a twenty-first century epidemic, and America's war on drugs is clearly directed at the wrong enemy." Dr. Joseph Mercola

By this point, you have learned about a vast array of tools that you'll be able to incorporate in your journey to a smoke-free life: from dietary changes to herbs, homeopathic remedies to nicotine replacement therapy. There is, of course, a giant elephant in the room that I've yet to discuss, and that elephant takes the form of pharmaceutical smoking cessation aids. Personally, I do not advocate taking this route.

Receptor blockers like **Chantix** are prescribed by some doctors to help people quit. This psychotropic drug is something I can't recommend however as some of its effects can be violence and suicide. It also gives many people terrifying nightmares.

I've met many people who used Chantix in the course of my work. Some were successful. Some quit and then started again after only a few weeks, but many had to stop taking it after only a few days or weeks because it was "making them crazy."

In my view, the potential downside is far too great to risk using such a drug, when there are other ways to quit which are much faster and cheaper in any case.

This is what it says on the www.chantix.com website:

"Some people have had changes in behavior, hostility, agitation, depressed mood, suicidal thoughts or actions while using CHANTIX to help them quit smoking. Some people had these symptoms when they began taking CHANTIX, and others developed them after several weeks of treatment or after stopping CHANTIX. If you, your family, or caregiver notice agitation, hostility, depression, or changes in behavior, thinking, or mood that are not typical for you, or you develop suicidal thoughts or actions, anxiety, panic, aggression, anger, mania, abnormal sensations, hallucinations, paranoia, or confusion, stop taking CHANTIX and call your doctor right away."

What concerns me here is what happens when someone else is not there to take control of you as you get caught up in paranoid or suicidal thoughts. In 2011, the Institute for Safe Medication Practices published that 272 people had committed suicide while taking Chantix. With this number of deaths, Chantix had more deaths associated with it than had any other monitored drug on the market at that time.

I think the possibility of committing suicide is already a deal breaker as far as choosing Chantix as an option goes, but in case you are not convinced, it goes on to say, *"Some people can have serious skin reactions while taking CHANTIX, some of which can become life-threatening. These can include rash, swelling, redness, and peeling of the skin. Some people can have allergic reactions to CHANTIX, some of which can be life-threatening and include: swelling of the face, mouth, and throat that can cause trouble breathing."*

Even if you are one of the lucky ones you are likely to feel pretty rotten: *"The most common side effects of CHANTIX include nausea (30%), sleep problems, constipation, gas and/or vomiting."*

"You may have trouble sleeping, vivid, unusual or strange dreams while taking CHANTIX." Many people I have met who have tried Chantix actually use the word *terrifying* when referring to the nightmares they experienced.

I don't know about you, but none of this sounds good to me.

Anti-depressants like **Wellbutrin,** which have been repackaged as **Zyban** for smoking cessation, can also be prescribed. Some people have been able to quit smoking after taking Wellbutrin because it can make you feel less anxious. Not being a proponent of pharmaceutical drugs I question as to what happens when you stop masking the issues causing the anxiety and depression, and come off the drug. I feel that EFT, hypnosis, or other therapy for depression or trauma are safer and more effective methods to deal with the psychological and emotional issues that reinforce the need to smoke. Disturbingly, two of the so-called side effects (I just call them effects) of Wellbutrin can also be extreme anxiety and depression despite what it's sold for.

Here are some excerpts of what is says on the www.wellbutrin.com website:

"WELLBUTRIN XL is not for everyone. There is a risk of seizure with WELLBUTRIN XL which increases with higher doses. Other side effects may include weight loss, dry mouth, nausea, difficulty sleeping, dizziness, sore throat, constipation, or flatulence.

In some children, teens, and young adults, antidepressants increase suicidal thoughts or actions."

My hope is that, given the serious risks associated with the pharmaceutical "aids" I've described, you will treat these drugs as your *very* last resort. In my work, time and again, I have found the natural way to be the most effective way, particularly when combined with techniques for releasing depression and anxiety. The risk inherent in pharmaceuticals is just not worth it. After all, you are trying to quit smoking in order to raise your vibration, not lower it. You are choosing to live not die.

Five-minute contemplation: "Smoking is not a loving act."

Chapter 19

What About e-Cigarettes?

"Big Tobacco must think all its Christmases have come at once. E-cigarettes may allow it to profit from nicotine addiction around the clock: in places (where and) *when you can't smoke, you should be able to vape, it argues."* Simon Chapman

Despite what the craftily created advertisements would have you believe, e-cigarettes are not a smoking cessation aid. That isn't to say that people haven't managed to quit using them, but I believe their success has more to do with resolve than the method used. By design e-cigarettes are not made to free you from nicotine addiction. After all if you quit nicotine you wouldn't buy their products anymore. In fact if you read the small print most of them will tell you so. If you really think about it, why would they? After all, you are keeping the same hand-to-mouth habit, and the nicotine is still causing your brain to be flooded with 200 neuro-chemicals all day long, just as it would with tobacco. All you have changed is the type of drug delivery device you are using.

There are now over 400 brands of e-cigarettes with the most popular like blu and VUSE owned by the tobacco companies Lorillard and Reynolds respectively. The industry as a whole is very excited as e-cigarettes carry a huge potential for creating new addicts, keeping the ones who want to break free from doing so, and even winning back some they had lost to quitting. This increasingly popular product also allows the tobacco companies to give the impression they "care" about their customers. The names Safe Cig, FreedomHealth, and Love-cigarette are good examples of marketing from the angle of being better for you. But are they?

E-cigarettes, at the time of writing, are unregulated and contain all kinds of ingredients. The main one of course is nicotine – often in very high doses. This spike of nicotine is just as powerful as that received from a cigarette (if not more so) and is what makes e-cigarettes so addictive. Not only that, but I've observed smokers sucking on their e-cigarette constantly, something you simply could not do with a cigarette. There are places where you can't or won't smoke but the e-cigarette has no limits. People use or "vape" them on planes, in restaurants, at work, and are even taking them to bed. This constant use raises the brain's baseline craving for nicotine. For the many smokers who try e-cigarettes for a while and then go back to cigarettes, they are horrified to discover that they now smoke more than ever!

The FDA[11] has also found the toxin diethylene glycol (used in anti-freeze) and the carcinogen nitrosamine in the cartridges of these high-tech devices. They have also been found to contain vegetable oils like mint oil, menthol oil, and cinnamon oil that, like all oils, when inhaled can cause lipoid pneumonia – especially when combined with plenty of warm water vapor. Already I have come across three people in my practice who ended up in the hospital with pneumonia after smoking e-

[11] Food and Drug Administration in the USA.

cigarettes for just a couple of months, and the doctor related it to using an e-cigarette. According to the National Cancer Institute, there is also emerging evidence that e-cigarettes are causing heart attacks and reducing the body's ability to fight disease.

With flavors like bubble gum, cotton candy, licorice, and butterscotch, and names like Wicked Honey and Wonka Sweet Tarts, it is clear that children are being targeted by the manufacturers. Many of these children would never have started to smoke cigarettes, but they are now addicted to nicotine because these cunning little devices are perceived as "cool" and "safe." Many companies are moving away from e-cigarettes that resemble their traditional carcinogenic counterparts and instead equipping their devices with a wide range of aesthetic flourishes. Some e-cigarettes have flashing lights down their lengths or glow blue at the tip; others produce dragon-style clouds of vapor or come with their own sleek, rechargeable carrying cases. Almost as exciting as a new iPhone! The vast majority of these children will have no idea that they are addicted until it's too late.

The reason children are targeted, and always have been, by the tobacco industry is that 88% of smokers start smoking before they are 18. "Get 'em young and keep 'em for life" is therefore the marketing policy!

The important thing to understand is that e-cigarettes are not designed to help you quit. They are designed to keep you addicted, and paying. Most people will try them for a while and then go back to smoking cigarettes as soon as they run out of cartridges, with perhaps a bout of pneumonia and a heart attack in the middle.

Five-minute contemplation: "I choose to raise my vibration far above that of nicotine addiction."

Chapter 20

Reward or Punishment?

"When I quit smoking I realized that I had used cigarettes as a reward system, my bonus for getting stuff done. Write this paragraph and you can have a cigarette. Clean the toilet and you can have a cigarette. Smoking was not only 'the monkey on my back' but I used it to motivate me to get through procrastination, tough jobs and unpleasant situations." FoundID.com

So, we've worked on ending the relationship and told our subconscious mind to send the demon away but there's still that little voice in your head that says, *"But I'll miss my little treat, my rewards, my little moments just for me."*

I see.

You've done well, you've exerted yourself, finished that last little chore, made it through a difficult day. Well done, great job.

Now imagine someone saying, "*Sit down and breathe in clouds of toxic chemicals as your reward. Bravo, inhale carbon monoxide! Go on, treat yourself to an early slow painful death.*"

Maybe there's a better way to reward yourself.

Maybe you could take a break, sit down with a cup of relaxing herb tea, breathe in fresh air, eat some blueberries, listen to some great music, be thankful for all the good things in your life, and give yourself a mental pat on the back. You are a good person; you've always done the best you could at the time. You deserve to be happy and healthy, not poisoned to death.[12]

Having a real reward can be a great motivator for quitting. Tell yourself that, after a few days of not smoking, you can have a new lipstick or a special kind of deluxe car wash. At the end of the first week of not smoking, consider treating yourself to a massage or a great meal. Think about what you can do to reward yourself with the extra time you have saved not smoking: soak in a hot bath full of essential oils by candlelight, chill out for an hour with a good book, or go and play with your children.

Then think of something that will be your reward at the end of the month and at the end of the year: a vacation, a better car, a new computer, a wonderful gift for someone you love. When you stop spending money on cigarettes, suddenly a whole new area of possible rewards opens up. Given you no longer need the money for cigarettes anymore it could even mean rewarding yourself with an easier work schedule.

Five-minute contemplation: "My success and the evolution of my soul sends ripples of joy across the web of consciousness."

---

[12] If by reading this, you realize that there is a part of you that is so hurt or so guilty that you really are using cigarettes to slowly kill yourself rather than "treat" yourself, now would be a good time to seek help to address the issue.

Chapter 21

Introducing Tapping

Not only are you going to quit smoking with this book but you are going to learn an invaluable technique that you can use for the rest of your life, both for improving your own sense of well-being and for helping friends and family.

At various points throughout the book I will refer to pre-set Tapping sequences which you can find on my website www.quitsmokingnowandforever.com. You can also use Tapping – or EFT, Emotional Freedom Technique – to release other emotions or even beliefs that you think could be hindering you from being smoke-free.

As far as quitting smoking, Tapping can help in a number of ways. It:

Eliminates the beliefs about smoking that keep us doing it despite knowing it's bad for us and wanting to stop.

Alleviates the withdrawal symptoms and cravings during the quitting process.

Releases the negative emotions that our smoking is trying merely to anesthetize, making smoking redundant.

Tapping is a technique that you can use to release anxiety and emotional pain throughout your life so that you never return to that low point where smoking seems like an option.

What is Tapping?

Tapping or Emotional Freedom Technique (EFT) was adapted from its Eastern medicine origins and formalized by Gary Craig. More recently the technique has been expanded upon by many healers who either focus on it entirely as a stand-alone therapy or integrate it into their existing healing practices. It is a process that changes dysfunctional beliefs and desensitizes painful emotions and memory.

The fingers are used to tap sequentially on acupressure points on various parts of the body, while focusing on a particular emotion or traumatic event. This is repeated until the negative emotion is entirely released. In the end, all you are left with is the "story." The related upset and anxiety are gone.

Tapping can also be used to release negative beliefs and physical pain or sickness.

Tapping is mostly known for its releasing effects, but it can also be used to reinforce positive affirmations and beliefs once the negative energy has been removed.

Although it is extremely helpful to have a professional guide you through a session, Tapping is something you can do by yourself with amazing results. In fact, it is something you can use on a daily basis for healing current issues as well as for clearing out old "baggage" from the past. It is very useful when trying to kick an addiction. To understand how it works it's useful to understand a little bit about energy.

We are Vibrating Energy

The whole Universe is made up of energy (light and dark). We and everything else are simply photon energy vibrating at a certain frequency. Some of this energy can be seen as material objects while other energy, like feelings or beliefs, cannot be seen but is just as real, despite vibrating at a frequency outside our limited band of sight and hearing.

Every emotion has a certain vibration. Positive emotions make you feel good and negative ones don't. Whether it is shame, humiliation, guilt, or grief at the bottom of the negative scale, or fear, craving, anger, or pride further up, it does not add to our sense of well-being. Negative beliefs (like "I'm useless" and "I can't quit") also act in the same way, making you feel worse.

Each person is made up of a set of different beliefs and emotions, both conscious and unconscious, which creates a kind of unique signature.

That then attracts things of a similar vibration to it. Ever wondered why angry people show up when you're in a bad mood, or why you end up seeing more sad things when you're in a funk? Now you know.

In the same way, when negative emotions are released, you feel lighter and are left with an overall higher frequency comprised of love, compassion, peace, and joy – which also attracts more of the things that make you feel good.

Cigarettes have a low frequency and are attracted to lower vibrations. As you raise your vibration, you and cigarettes are no longer a good fit and they will fall away from your life. In the same way, as you quit smoking, your vibration increases and attracts more positive things into your life.

Tapping gets rid of the anxiety and fear that keep you stuck in an imagined future, and releases the sadness and depression that keep you stuck in the past. It allows you to live in the Now. This is when life really gets to be fun!

How does Tapping work?

The fingers tap specific points on the body while the emotion is verbally described. The tapping series is performed until the negative emotion is completely removed, leaving only the "story." All the sadness, nervousness, or whatever is gone. Tapping can also be used to release negative beliefs and physical pain or sickness.

Not only that, but it is gone forever. This is not temporary relief. The energy of the negative emotion has been transmuted. Cravings for cigarettes, alcohol, or drugs cease. Often the effects of Tapping can seem almost miraculous.

There are three powerful Tapping sessions related to smoking at the end of the book, which you can also follow along to online at www.quitsmokingnowandforever.com.

Five-minute contemplation: "My emotions are an aspect of my mind but I am not my mind."

Chapter 22

Breathe Fresh Air

"Be aware of your breathing. Notice how this takes attention away from your thinking and creates space." Eckhart Tolle

Unless you have the misfortune to live in places like Dzerzhinsk, Russia or Linfen, China (two of the top ten most polluted cities in the world apparently), it has got to be better to just breathe deeply than to take psychotropic drugs or use an alternative drug delivery device like the e-cigarette, to help with quitting.

When I ask people what, of all the things I told them to do, really helped the most, almost everyone says "the breathing."

"*Breathing*?" you might ask, "*but I do that all the time.*" Well yes you do, but most people don't breathe in the right way. They tend to breathe very shallowly, and more and more so as they get more uptight and anxious – which actually perpetuates the anxious feeling.

Ironically, when you draw deeply on a cigarette, you are breathing in a way that lowers anxiety and stress. The only trouble is that you are breathing in toxic chemicals and releasing adrenaline at the same time, which will later cause even more anxiety.

When you just breathe fresh air deeply in through your nose (expanding your rib cage and raising your diaphragm), hold it for a few seconds, and then breathe out slowly through your mouth, your body releases endorphins. The effect is to immediately slow your heart rate, lower your blood pressure, and make you feel calm and centered.

Smoking each cigarette usually involves about 8-10 puffs. When you experience a nicotine craving, if you simply take a little "non-cigarette" break and breathe in fresh air, 8-10 times in the way I've just described, you will suddenly find that the anxiety and irritation you were feeling just disappears. It is faster acting than any drug and has no nasty side effects, not to mention being free!

Practice this kind of breathing straight away. It will help enormously with getting free of nicotine, but it will also help you deal with negative emotions throughout your entire life. Many cigarette smokers have never learned an alternative method to stop feeling "bad" because they have always been able to anesthetize themselves with a cigarette.

Breathe in deeply and slowly through the nose, raise the diaphragm, hold it for a few seconds, and then breathe out slowly and fully through pursed lips – as if you are breathing out a great plume of steam on an icy day!

In Chapter 31 I will describe another breathing technique which is even more powerful at transmuting negative energy and emotions. It's called "Breathing in the Love."

Now that you are nice and relaxed from this basic breathing, say to yourself, "*I am ready and willing to release this need for cigarettes.*"

Say it again, louder, and with more feeling, *"I am ready and willing to release this need for cigarettes."*

One more time, "*I AM READY AND WILLING TO RELEASE THIS NEED FOR CIGARETTES, RIGHT NOW!*"

Great! Now let's set the stage for success.

Five-minute contemplation: "The breath of life is in me."

Chapter 23

The Day Before

"Your clothes smell heavily of clothing. Your den is filled with low-hanging palls of fresh air. The only rattle in your car is the sound of the toll change in the ashtray. The absence of the telltale tobacco stains on your shirt collar tells the tale – you've licked the smoking habit." Robert Brault, 1973

So here we are – on the brink of freedom.

We'll start with a writing exercise that will help you visualize your goals, an integral first step in achieving them. After that, we're going to choose some alternative behaviors and rewards for you to adopt during the quitting process. Lastly, we'll go over a list of purchases and logistics to be taken care of before embarking on your first day towards freedom. Let's begin.

A great way to begin this task is to write down your **personal goal about quitting**. Write it in the present tense and include all the great benefits you will have achieved as well as how it will make you feel. Using the word *grateful* in any statement of intention is always incredibly powerful.

It could go something like this:

> *It is* (future date) *and I am so happy and grateful to be a non-smoker. I am entirely free of cigarettes. I look 10 years younger, I smell good, I can breathe more easily and I have lots more energy. My [father, mother, wife, brother, friend] is so pleased that I no longer smoke. I have saved $____ already from not smoking which means I can now afford__________________.*

Write it down and put it up somewhere so you can read it every day. When you do read it, really visualize yourself as the new non-smoking you. Feel how relieved you feel and how much your self-esteem has gone up. Feel it and see it and be grateful, as if it's already happened.

Set up a positive trigger

You have been using smoking as an artificial way to release "happy" chemicals like dopamine, so let's set up a natural way for you to be able to do that yourself. I want you to find a quiet place and listen on the website or read through the following visualization. Practice deep breathing as you do this.

Allow yourself to remember a time when you felt really good, really safe, really happy: almost blissful. Create it as vividly as possible; see it, feel it, hear it, smell it. If you can't think of a time like this, imagine what it would be like. Focus on that pleasurable feeling in your body and turn it way up, making it as intense as possible. Now keep playing it over and over and as you do so, squeeze your thumb and index finger together. Make the images bright, the sounds loud and harmonious, the feelings strong and intense. We are creating an association between your feeling of pleasure and the squeezing of your fingers.

Now stop and relax, and then do it two more times.

Once the pleasurable feeling is firmly anchored, stop and take a few easy breaths before squeezing your fingers together again. You should feel that feeling of pleasure course through your body.

Now imagine yourself in various situations where you would normally smoke. For instance, first thing in the morning: imagine yourself getting up, having breakfast, and not smoking. Press your fingers together and allow that good feeling to get linked to not smoking when you get up. Do the same for the experience of not smoking a cigarette with coffee, with a beer, watching a football game, taking a break at work. See yourself in those situations (without a cigarette) and press your fingers together. Imagine someone offering you a cigarette and you saying, "No thanks, I don't smoke," as you press your fingers together. How great it feels to say no!

You can press your fingers together and trigger this good feeling whenever you need to. Use it to gain mastery over the craving.

Stock up for success

Get your patches and/or lobelia if you've decided to use them and perhaps some herbs for sleeping, like chamomile or valerian root.[13] If you have chosen not to use nicotine patches, using the herb mucuna pruriens and lobelia together is very effective.

- Decide if you are going to use some of the homeopathic remedies to help reduce the withdrawal symptoms and if you do, go and buy them. You could also wait a few days and see if you need any additional

[13] The hormone melatonin works well for sleeping and is good for anti-aging too!

help. If you can't afford them right away, you will be able to after a few days of cutting down and not spending so much on cigarettes.

- Consider buying some good quality vitamins and minerals to start repairing your body.

- Make a decision to eat healthily. Buy lots of organic fruit and vegetables and stock up the fridge with good fresh things you can easily eat when your blood sugar gets a bit low.

- Clean up and put away all your ashtrays. Make a statement of your intention to the universe, by throwing away your lighter.

- Put a sticker on your pack of cigarettes saying "*I am a non-smoker*" and then put the pack away, say in the garage, under the sink in the bathroom, or in the trunk of the car. Choose somewhere that makes it inconvenient to get them, and well out of sight. Later you will be able to get rid of them completely. If it feels okay to get rid of them now, go right ahead.

- Make sure you have real food for breakfast like oatmeal with almond milk and a banana or a boiled egg and wholegrain toast with perhaps some green tea instead of coffee.

- If you live with a partner who has decided to continue smoking, you need to be mindful of the triggers and obstacles that lie ahead. It might be a difficult or awkward conversation, but you need to sit down with your partner and establish ground rules. If the taste of tobacco on your partner's breath makes you anxious or sparks cravings, he/she might need to brush his/her teeth before kissing you. If you and your partner used to discuss your workdays and "bond" over evening cigarettes, you need to develop a new ritual.

- Do the Tapping session for 'Fear of Quitting,' which you can either follow along with on the website or read yourself as you tap along. You'll find it at the end of the book.
- At bedtime listen to the 'Quit Smoking Forever' MP3 through headphones which you can also find at :

www.quitsmokingnowandforever.com

Five-minute contemplation: "I consciously weave this new non-smoking me into being."

Chapter 24

One Day at a Time

"The best thing about the future is that it comes one day at a time." Abraham Lincoln

Day One

Get up and immediately brush your teeth and have a shower. Notice how good it feels to have a fresh mouth and clean skin. Congratulate yourself for embarking on this process to be free.

If you are using them, stick on the patch or patches that are right for you and/or take a drop or pinch of lobelia in your cheek. If you have purchased homeopathic remedies or flower remedies, wait to use them a half an hour or so after brushing your teeth or using the lobelia.

Eat breakfast, even if it's just fruit, a smoothie, or a protein bar. Sit somewhere different than you normally would. Use a different cup. Remember that coffee is acidic and will neutralize the nicotine patch if you are using one, making you crave a tobacco "fix." Green tea would be better as it still gives you a caffeine boost but is alkaline. It also contains antioxidants that help clear out dangerous free radicals from your body.

Do ten rounds of the deep breathing exercise. Breathe in through the nose, raise your diaphragm as high as you can, hold for five seconds, and then breathe out slowly from pursed lips. You can count off each breath on your fingers to keep track.

Your job today is to smoke as few cigarettes as possible.

Take five minutes and do this visualization process: *Close your eyes for a moment and imagine three foods or liquids that you really dislike. For instance, pig's liver, semolina pudding, steamed brains or sweetbreads, anchovies, lukewarm sour milk, the snotty bit of an egg, or grilled cockroaches! Then imagine these three horrible things all roughly chopped and mixed together. Look at them in your mind. Smell it, and then imagine putting a large spoonful into your mouth. Chew it slowly, feel the texture...swallow it...and really feel how nauseous it makes you feel. Makes you want to gag. Now when this feeling is at its peak, imagine lighting a cigarette and sucking that toxic smoke into your body. Sucking it in, swallowing it down. Imagine smoking with friends, imagine smoking when you first wake up, imagine smoking in your breaks......... Oh yes, it feels so good right? (Not). Drink a glass of cool fresh water and take a few deep breaths. Do it a couple more times. Be happy you don't have to smoke!*

Immediately go to work, or start your day with an activity or relaxing walk. Take a big bottle of water, with a lime or lemon juice in it, along with an apple, yogurt, some nuts, or a carrot to snack on later. Sodas like Coke, Sprite, Fanta, or Mountain Dew would be a poor choice as they are extremely acidic. Apart from risking making you ill in the future they will neutralize the patch and prevent it from doing its job. They act as excellent cleaning products for engines however.

You have to eat regularly to keep your blood sugar on a nice even keel. In the past you have relied on nicotine to release blood sugar.

Now you are going to rely on real food, full of nutrients which can repair cells and keep you healthy, as well as give you the energy you need.

Use the lobelia every hour or two, or whenever you have a craving.

Practice the deep breathing whenever smoking comes into your mind or you feel stressed.

Drink lots of water.

Keep repeating to yourself "***I am*** *a non-smoker*" despite wanting or even having a cigarette.

Take breaks during the day. Not stinky cigarette breaks, just breaks to rest, relax, and breathe in some fresh air.

In the beginning it may be wise to stay away from the company of smokers. Some may seriously want you to quit and will support you, while others will want to sabotage you so as not to lose a smoking buddy. It's hard to raise your own vibration when surrounded by others who are not on the same path. If you want to be a non-smoker, be around non-smokers.

In the evening, if you drink alcohol, consider stopping for a few weeks or cutting down. Know that after a couple of drinks "Silly Thirteen-Year-Old You" will come out and you will forget all about why you are quitting or even that you are quitting at all!

Congratulate yourself for cutting down. It was easier than you thought maybe?

Before bed listen to the 'Quit Smoking Forever' MP3 again.

Day Two

Get up and immediately brush your teeth and have a shower.

Stick on the patch or patches or take lobelia and perhaps some mucuna if you feel a bit down in the dumps.

Eat breakfast, even if it's just fruit, a smoothie, oatmeal, or a cheese sandwich. Drink your green tea, which contains caffeine and plenty of antioxidants to fight cancer and disease. It will help you stay slim.

No smoking in the house or car. If you feel at all nauseous during your commute, pack a thermos of ginger tea to drink while you're driving.

Throughout the day use one drop or pinch of lobelia in your cheek. It will make you feel like you just had a cigarette.

Repeat the deep breathing exercise ten times.

Complete this little visualization process. Once you have read it through, close your eyes and begin.

Imagine yourself in a couple of months from now. You are getting ready to go out for dinner with someone, for a special occasion. You are standing in front of a mirror and you notice how good you look. Your skin is smoother, your hair is shinier, your eyes are brighter, and you look happier than you have been in a very long time. You notice how much easier it is to breathe, and how it's been weeks since you coughed or wheezed. You feel that vital energy in your body and realize how far you have come. You no longer smoke, you are no longer addicted to nicotine… you are free. Finally free. Enjoy how good that feels. Feel proud of yourself. You deserve some acknowledgement. You did a great thing, a difficult thing, and you were successful. Smile at that image of yourself in the mirror and take that feel-good feeling with you for the rest of the day. You <u>are</u> a non-smoker.

Immediately go to work, or start your day with an activity or a walk. Take a big bottle of lime or lemon water, along with a snack like an oatmeal bar or banana for later.

Decide what to do after lunch. Perhaps have a mint tea? Perhaps go for a quick walk? Do the breathing. Use a drop of lobelia.

Don't go outside with the smoking gang during breaks at work. It's important that you put old rituals and habits to rest. It's fine to chat with your smoker friends around the water cooler or in the cafeteria, but watching them light up might cause anxiety and temptation – the opposite of what you need!

Make sure you have a snack for mid-afternoon.

Remember the lobelia. Check now and again that your patch is still on if you are using one.

Don't get bored. Keep yourself busy. Write a list of things to do when you have a period of inactivity: anything from finally organizing your jewelry drawer or toolbox, finishing that model car you always wanted to make, or doing the crossword in the paper during a moment of inactivity at work.

Prepare a healthy organic dinner.

If you are feeling miserable and are not already using the mucuna bean extract, consider using it. It is a very effective mood enhancer.

If you live with people who smoke, ask them to smoke outside, away from you, and to keep their packs of cigarettes out of sight. Thank them for being supportive. Let's hope they find your efforts an inspiration to stop too.

Use a "sleepy" tea at bedtime and visualize the next day without cigarettes.

Do the 'Tapping for Craving' session which you can watch on the website or read at the end of the book.

Listen to the hypnosis session again before going to bed.

If you are still smoking at all, work out how many cigarettes you smoked today compared with an average day before your decision to quit. Give yourself a pat on the back and decide to go for fewer tomorrow. As soon as you go a whole day without smoking this will be your First Day of Freedom. You are doing great!

Day Three

Get up and immediately brush your teeth and have a shower.

Stick on the patch or patches if you are using them or use lobelia or homeopathic remedies.

Eat breakfast. Drink your green tea (or a small coffee if you can't bear to give it up completely). Remember no fizzy drinks or orange juice. Apple or cherry, etc. is fine. Even grapefruit is good as just like limes and lemons, the body renders it alkaline.

Take five minutes and imagine the following scenario:

The idea of having a cigarette pops into your head. It's like being at a junction. Do I go right or left? To the right is an archway, all lit up like Las Vegas: flashing neon lights, music, exotic cocktails, dancing girls, gambling, and a promise of instant gratification. You think, "Wow, that looks like fun," *and off you go, lighting your cigarette as you go. For ten minutes you walk on the Vegas Strip until suddenly it starts to get dark, it starts to feel cold, the streets get dirtier, grayer, and uglier. You see endless concrete, poverty, sickness, vomit, and smell stale urine in this place behind the façade. You are shocked, scared, and you think,* "What is this place, how did I get here? I never knew it was like this." *You pray for salvation.*

Go back to the junction. Look to the left. There is no cigarette. It's not that exciting. In fact it looks a little daunting with a rather large pile of rocks blocking the way. You put on your boots and your patches, take a drop of lobelia, and clamber over the rocks. You do the breathing exercises and drink plenty of water and keep on climbing. Once on the other side it suddenly opens out into the most beautiful scenery. There is the ocean on one side, turquoise blue and sparkling, and a meadow on the other, green and lush. There are bunny rabbits and birds and wild flowers of all kinds. The sun is shining and you feel so good. You breathe to yourself, "I am so glad to be alive! I am so glad I chose the right path!" *You do a funny little dance for the joy of it all.*

Make sure, if you still have that pack of toxic cigarettes, that they are tucked away out of sight with that big sticker on them saying "I AM a non-smoker!" If you feel strong enough, throw them away after soaking them in water. After all, you don't want to find yourself rooting around in the trash later for a broken piece. It's so humiliating!

Use one drop or pinch of lobelia in your cheek.

Repeat the deep breathing exercise ten times.

Make a plan to do something that you really like today: something that will increase your natural dopamine that has been depleted for so long by nicotine use. It could be something like watching the sunset or a funny movie or spending time with people who make you happy.

Immediately go to work, or start your day with an activity or a walk. Take your water along with an apple, dark chocolate, yogurt, some nuts, or an oatmeal cookie for a snack later.

If anxiety or irritation comes to the surface, walk away and do the breathing exercises. Focus on what the emotion feels like. You will immediately calm down. Remind yourself that no one has ever died of a craving, no one's head has ever exploded from a desire to smoke, and in a couple of minutes it *will* pass. Use some Bach's Flower Remedy.

If you find yourself distracted by thoughts of smoking shout "*STOP*" and visualize a large stop sign in your head and it will end those obsessive thoughts. I told one lady to do this and she used to shout it out loud in the street, which got some funny looks, but she said she didn't care because it stopped her from smoking. The fact is it's important to be prepared to do whatever it takes.

If you do smoke a cigarette, limit it to three puffs and then put it out. It will be enough to stop the craving. Why add more tar and toxins to your body? It's best to throw the half-smoked cigarette away, but if you decide to smoke the rest later, make sure you cut the end off first. The burnt end is even more carcinogenic when re-lit. Forgive yourself for not being stronger and tell yourself that this will be the last!

Use the lobelia regularly. It stops the craving and interferes with the nicotine, helping to un-addict you. It's better to use it regularly at the beginning to prevent cravings rather than wait until you get the craving.

Repeat over and over to yourself, *"I am a non-smoker. Even if I still have a craving for a cigarette sometimes, I AM a non-smoker."* Insist upon it. "I AM" is the name of God. It's a very powerful statement.

Drink lots of water. It helps reduce craving, hydrates you, and helps eliminate all the built-up toxins in your body.

Go for a walk for at least 15 minutes. It releases stress and helps kick-start your metabolism into returning to normal. Take it slow at the beginning and then increase your pace and time as it gets easier over the next few weeks.

Congratulate yourself for cutting down further, or for quitting smoking if this is already the case. Don't worry if you are not quite there yet. Everyone has a different pattern for quitting.

Have a hot bath with Epsom salts or a hot shower and imagine all those cigarette toxins coming out of your body.

Plan your day tomorrow, making sure you have everything you need, and listen to the hypnosis MP3 again before sleeping. It's okay if you fall asleep listening to it, as the subconscious mind is still taking it in.

Day Four

Get up and immediately brush your teeth and have a shower. Notice how much better you feel already. Notice how much more confident you feel about conquering this demon once and for all.

Stick on the patch or patches or use the lobelia.

Eat breakfast.

Remember to change your routine: sit in a different chair, stay in if you normally go outside, put on some relaxing music, save the newspaper for later – or never. If listening to the news on television makes you feel anxious, give yourself a respite: pick up a novel from the library or just sit and enjoy the luxury of just "being."

Think about the things in your life that are stressing you out. Consider making some changes in your life. Maybe certain people are no good for you anymore. Maybe you should go for a different job? An easy way to know is to close your eyes, think about the person or circumstance and notice if the energy in your body increases or diminishes. If it goes down you know it's time to go in another direction.

And the things that you can't change, stop worrying about them. Your worry is putting attention onto the negative and will create more of the same. Take a deep breath. Have faith. All will be well.

If you have not achieved this already, start thinking about making today the one you go all day without a cigarette. Be very clear you are not going to have that first cigarette and then keep putting it off until the end of the day. Then turn in for an early night!

Use one drop or pinch of lobelia in your cheek.

Repeat the deep breathing exercise ten times.

Start increasing your aerobic exercise: walking, cycling, swimming, etc. Think about going to the gym or starting yoga in a class or online.

Remember to take your big bottle of water with some food to keep your blood sugar balanced during the day.

If you feel anxious or irritated, walk away and do the breathing exercise. You will immediately calm down. Remind yourself again that no one has ever died of a craving, and in a couple of minutes it will pass. Remember, withdrawal symptoms have been designed to make you feel as if something bad is going to happen, but in reality nothing will happen – apart from you breaking away from the chains of addiction of course!

Keep the lobelia in your pocket and use it every 1-2 hours.

Repeat over and over to yourself, *"I am a non-smoker," "I don't smoke – no matter what,"* and *"Smoking is not an option."* Decide that regardless of how you feel, you simply won't give in to that nicotine demon trying to get back into your head. Defeat him once and for all. Banish him forever. You are now in charge of your life and you choose to be healthy, happy, and free!

Remember to shout "STOP" in your head if a little wheedling voice comes up with reasons you should smoke.

Drink lots of water. As you drink it, imagine all that tar and poison being washed from your body.

Congratulate yourself for how far you have come. Allow that confidence to build up inside of you. You can do this. You are doing it.

Day Five

"Don't be discouraged. It's often the last key in the bunch that opens the lock." Anonymous

Do your new morning routine with breakfast and the patch and/or lobelia.

Practice the breathing exercise. It's important to do it often because it helps you stay calm. It is also vital that you make it part of your way of life. In the future – whether it is weeks, months, or even years into your reclaimed life as a non-smoker – there will come a stressful time when you may be tempted to smoke unless you have another technique at the ready to relieve the stress. As a smoker you were using nicotine to suppress negative emotions rather than release them, and now it's time to start using a more helpful technique. The really wonderful thing about breathing is it has no downside.

If you haven't already, spend a few moments and write a "Dear John" letter to your cigarettes, similar to the examples I included in Chapter 8. Tell your "ex-lover" and so-called "friend" that although you had some good times you've realized what a dangerous destructive relationship it is. Give all the reasons why you have to break it off and make it very clear that it is absolutely over, forever. There will be no coming back this time. Kicking this addiction really is like ending a toxic relationship. It is nerve-wracking at the time but there is such a sense of relief after you've done it. Imagine you have put a court restraining order on that little demon too. Lock the windows and doors of your mind to him forever.

Take the lobelia, some food, and water with you when you leave the house. You are not going to be eating more, just spreading your food out more evenly throughout the day and choosing healthier options. If you are addicted to sodas or energy drinks use the same technique as for cigarettes and wean yourself off them over a few days using an alternative like iced green tea, coconut water, or juice.

Use the positive trigger technique, where your press your thumb and index finger together, to keep yourself feeling good.

Keep repeating your mantra, *"I AM a non-smoker."* Put up signs around the house and in your car reinforcing the same thing. Tell your friends and family you don't smoke. Forget using words like "trying" to quit. The word "trying" can keep you trapped forever not quite achieving your goal.

Congratulate yourself on your success to date. If you have stopped smoking, that's great! If you have cut down just keep going using everything you have learned so far. You may need a few more days but you are getting there.

Onwards and Upwards

"Many of life's failures are people who did not realize how close they were to success when they gave up." Thomas Edison

If you are still smoking a few, just repeat the instructions I've given you over the past few days until you stop completely. Look at what it is that's still trying to sabotage you. Have you transformed your home into that of a non-smoker, getting rid of all ashtrays and lighters? Are you socializing with people who undermine your attempts to quit, whether intentionally or unintentionally? Are you permitting negative emotions or self-talk to dominate your thoughts?

If you get stuck, consider using more of the patches or other forms of NRT. Even though it's toxic in large amounts, the nicotine itself is not the thing that kills you, it's all the rest of the stuff, so don't worry about using it now to break the habit of smoking.

If you have not tried the lobelia, try it. If you have not tried the mucuna, try that. You will be surprised at how well they work. If you have not tried the homeopathic remedies, try some. By this point you will have a better idea of which remedies apply to you.

Remember the cigarette manufacturers have added 599 additives to keep you hooked physically and chemically and spent billions of dollars in marketing to keep you brainwashed mentally and socially. At this point you need to use all the weapons at your disposal in order to win the war.

Keep listening to the hypnosis session and do the Tapping sessions.

Here are some other motivational strategies to consider.

If you are someone who responds better to the stick than the carrot, you could try a slap on the wrist. Get an elastic band and wear it around your wrist. Whenever you have a thought about smoking pull it out and let it snap back on your wrist. *Ouch! Naughty thought! Bad idea!* Well, whatever works, right?

Commit yourself again. Remind yourself why you want to quit. Write the reasons down, if you haven't already, and stick them on your fridge. Keep going.

If having money is a good motivator for you, start putting the money that you are saving by not smoking in a jar, and then keep on going once you stop the cigarettes completely. You'll be amazed at how satisfying $200 looks in fives and ones!

If lack of money and your personal honor is a motivator, tell someone you will give them $100 (or whatever is appropriate) if you don't keep your word to become a non-smoker.

As you round out the first five days here is some more coaching advice to get you through the next stage of becoming a non-smoker.

If you are using the patches (and not just lobelia) it's a good idea to go for between 7-14 days after stopping smoking on *the same amount of nicotine patch you used in the beginning*. It acts like a safety harness while you practice being a non-smoker. As each day goes by your nicotine receptors are slowly changing to need less nicotine. You may have stopped smoking, but you aren't out of the woods quite yet. One 21mg patch is equivalent to 11 cigarettes' worth of nicotine and it's extremely hard to go from that, to nothing, overnight. Like most addictive drugs you need to wean yourself off slowly.

After the 7-14 days of not smoking it's time to cut the patches down by third or half. If you have been using one 21mg patch then move down to the 14mg patch. Then, after two weeks, go down to 7mg and keep using this last patch for another 7-14 days. At this point your body will be completely weaned off nicotine and you will be both cigarette and nicotine free. Hurrah!

If you are using the lobelia alone, continue to use it regularly for at least 4 days after you stop smoking. Don't worry about using it. It is non-addictive despite its similarity to tobacco. You can continue to use the lobelia while you wean off the patches, as it will help speed up the process a little. The mucuna will help a lot too, and can be taken for a few months, elevating your mood and keeping you up there until all of the depressing effects of cigarettes have worn off.

The trick at this stage is not to get impatient and stop following the plan too soon. Unless of course you have suddenly become enlightened and realize that you already are, in fact, a perfect, healthy, free non-smoker: always have been and always will be. In which case you are done!

Five-minute contemplation: "I exist in the energy web of all potential and am one with it."

Chapter 25

Keeping You on Track

"If you are going through hell, keep going." Winston Churchill

People who take their time are much more likely to be successful. It's like learning anything; it takes a while to really stick. It's said to take 21 days to really change a habit. If you don't engage the magic of metaphysics of course – in which case it happens instantaneously!

You are now learning how to be a non-smoker, after years of programming and low level emotions that kept you being the opposite. You are also learning how to remain a non-smoker, and the No.1 rule for that is not to smoke. It sounds obvious, but the little demon can play marvelous tricks. He can say things like, "*Well you've been quit a month now, you deserve a cigarette*" or "*Now that you've been quit six months, I wonder what one would taste like.*" It sounds ridiculous but so many people have fallen for it.

Cheating on your diet may be okay at Christmas (after all, you are not going to suddenly put on fifty pounds after eating one piece of cake); however, cheating with a cigarette takes you right back to the miserable addiction of nicotine. There is no "cheating" or having a secret affair on the side when it comes to the nicotine demon – he just moves right back in.

Smoking "just one," or even having a puff, is like landing on the second-to-last square on the "Chutes and Ladders" board.[14] You slide straight back down to the start of the game.

You were the one who decided to quit, and you have succeeded. Don't let anything come between you and that success. You deserve to be free. You do not deserve to be a smoker with all the negativity that it entails.

You are not missing anything by the way. Have you lost a job opportunity, a friend, the love of your life, a home, your health, your looks, or your life through being a non-smoker? Name one thing that you have lost by not smoking. Can't think of any? Me neither.

Life is difficult? It may well be right now, but how on earth will being addicted to cigarettes again make it any better?

You are now no longer a pitiful slave. You are a free person with restored health and confidence and more ability to deal with life's ups and downs than ever before.

You have your dignity back, your health back, your freedom and your mind back. Never choose to give them up.

You deserve to be healthy, happy, and free.

Never become complacent. Never forget how it felt to be a smoker and how vastly improved your life now is. Sometimes we can look back at things with rose-colored glasses.

Look at the smokers you see around you. Notice how silly it looks to puff on a little white roll of dead leaves. Notice how trapped and controlled smoking keeps them, how their skin has a gray pallor, how

---

[14] Also known as Snakes and Ladders.

stressed and nervous they seem if they can't get a "fix." Notice the lines around their lips and how horrible they smell. Notice how they have to persuade themselves as to how much they "love" smoking so as not to admit they are just addicted to nicotine.

Notice all of this and feel compassion for them. Feel grateful that this is no longer you. The dark fog has lifted. Keep walking in the sunlight.

Five-minute contemplation: "We are the creators of the program of life."

Chapter 26

Quitting Smoking with No Weight Gain

"I've got two daughters who will have to make their way in this skinny-obsessed world, and it worries me, because I don't want them to be empty-headed, self-obsessed, emaciated clones; I'd rather they were independent, interesting, idealistic, kind, opinionated, original, funny – a thousand things, before thin." J.K. Rowling

Many people worry they are going to put on a lot of weight when they quit smoking, and you may be one of them. It does not have to be that way though.

You've no doubt experienced how smoking dampens your appetite, allowing you to miss meals. Smoke also damages your taste buds, which makes food less appealing, and slightly increases the rate at which your body burns calories (by about 100 extra a day).

Because of this, and the fact that it takes a while for the body to regain its normal balance, many people put on some weight when they quit – usually between 5-10 pounds. For some it is significantly more. Carrying a few extra pounds, however, is not nearly as dangerous as smoking, and there are many things you can do to stay slim that don't end up killing you.

Most of the weight gain is usually due to an increase in eating and this can be for many reasons. Some people want to eat more because it tastes so good once they've quit. If this is your case, just take one helping and tell yourself you'll have more later on if you really need it. Remember too that if fattening foods are not around, you won't eat them. Rather like cigarettes really – if they aren't around you can't smoke them.

As you quit you may find yourself wanting to indulge in sweet things in an attempt to relieve some of the withdrawal symptoms. Sugar causes a spike of energy, rather like nicotine does, but it then crashes shortly after, making you feel worse. Be careful not to swap a cigarette addiction for a sugar addiction. It is highly acidic and creates an environment in your body for disease to flourish. If you can stay off it for a while you will no longer crave it. Fake sugar is even worse. Just look up the effects of Aspartame[15] on your body and you will see what I mean. It's shocking.

It's important to keep your blood sugar very stable while quitting, but rather than adding snacks to what you are already eating at meal times, spread the food out. For instance eat half your lunchtime sandwich at one o'clock, and save the other half to eat at at four o'clock in the afternoon. Having mini-meals like this also helps you stay slim.

Sometimes the willpower it takes to resist smoking may make passing up sweets and other tempting foods more challenging. Don't believe the voice in your head when it says, *"You've given up smoking;*

---

[15] Now called AminoSweet in an attempt to pass under the radar of people trying to avoid it.

you deserve a cream-filled donut to fill that space." It is lying! It lies about everything.

If you feel a little empty, imagine that space being filled up with love or joy instead, and remember you have not "given up" anything by ditching cigarettes. After all what is there to give up? Can you think of one thing that you would not be better off without? Becoming a non-smoker is ALL positive.

Find other ways to feel good. Eating calorie-laden food usually ends up making you feel sluggish, so go for a walk in the park, in the woods, or on the beach, spend time with friends, play with your pets or children, watch a funny movie, watch the sunrise, list all the things you are grateful and thankful for, help someone less fortunate than you are, or take up a new hobby. In this way you create your own dopamine, naturally, without having to eat to get it.

Some people reach for food instead of a cigarette when they feel stressed or bored. Watch for this and do some deep breathing and keep yourself busy. Clean out those kitchen drawers filled with goodness knows what, and throw away all the old ashtrays while you're at it!

Be sure to exercise. In addition to burning calories, exercise reduces withdrawal symptoms by releasing endorphins. If you are new to exercise, take it slowly. If you have been smoking for a few years expect to encounter some shortness of breath. All people starting new regimens must get through the rocky beginning, and those rocks feel a little bigger when scaled with damaged lungs. As your lungs and body get stronger though, you'll find you have more stamina. Walking is a great way to ease yourself into it. Exercise that was once a chore will become an enjoyable part of your day and assure you get a good night's sleep.

Not all people who smoke are necessarily slim to start with of course. Despite an increased metabolism, people who smoke heavily – more than 25 cigarettes a day – are more likely to be overweight or obese than people who smoke fewer cigarettes. It's hard to get motivated to exercise when you are so lacking in oxygen! Smoking can also increase insulin resistance and cause fat to be stored around the waist. This is also why smoking causes diabetes by the way. Releasing sugar into the system hundreds of times a day eventually causes the pancreas to shut down.

Get to the root of the problem. If you notice yourself having a compulsion to eat, look at what the root of that might be. What are you trying to stuff down? What don't you want to feel? What's eating at you? Maybe now is the right time to get help with resolving those issues.

Visualize a better you. Rather than worrying about getting fat, use visualizations to imagine yourself slim. See yourself standing in front of a mirror. See how your clothes are loose and how good you look. Remember, *"What we think about, comes about."*

Apart from the esthetic and health issues of weight gain, you definitely don't want to find yourself being fooled into smoking again just to lose the excess weight you put on – that would be a disaster. To make sure this does not happen here are a few other tools to help you keep the weight off:

Lobelia (Indian Tobacco), as we have mentioned before, is so similar to tobacco that it too releases fats and converts them to blood sugar. It also releases a little adrenaline, keeping your metabolism higher. I know many ex-smokers who have put on no weight at all, by simply using lobelia throughout the day as they quit. One drop in the cheek of the tincture or 1/5 of a capsule of the powdered herb every 1-2 hours is all you need.

Mucuna pruriens is another herb reported to help you keep weight off, as it increases the amount of dopamine in your brain, ensuring you don't eat to cheer yourself up.

Green tea contains plenty of caffeine and is good for burning fat; it is alkaline and possesses great antioxidant properties. You can drink it hot or iced, or even add the dry leaf to smoothies!

Herbal teas, essential oils, or capsules made from dandelion, milk thistle, ginseng, or peppermint all help in weight control in various ways.

The Hay Diet is a great way to stay slim. No, you don't eat hay! It advocates not mixing meat with carbohydrates like rice, pasta, bread, or potatoes in the same meal, making the digestive process far more efficient so less fat is stored. If you feel like pasta for lunch have it with a tomato sauce or mushrooms. If you want roast chicken for dinner have it with green beans and a salad.

Eat Right for your Type is a way of eating according to your blood type which also allows you to become, and remain, lean. As an example, if you are type A and eat meat, it turns to fat. If you are type O, meat gets turned into energy and you stay slim. You can buy the books pertaining to both of these great ways of eating on my website: www.quitsmokingnowandforever.com.

Always remember that even if you do end up putting on a few pounds, it's easier to lose them than deal with potential cancer or heart disease.

Five-minute contemplation: "I suppose nothing to be impossible for me."

Chapter 27

Note for Recovering Alcoholics and Drug Addicts

"My rule of life prescribed as an absolutely sacred rite [is] smoking cigars and also the drinking of alcohol before, after and if need be during all meals and in the intervals between them." Winston Churchill

Drinking alcohol is often associated with smoking, acting as a trigger. As the alcohol takes effect it erodes the commitment to quit. At a certain point of inebriation that commitment is entirely forgotten. An alcoholic will find it very hard to quit smoking until they become sober. Once sober, however, it's a lot easier to quit smoking, and interestingly this in turn helps you stay sober.

It is now clear from studies[16] that quitting smoking increases your chances of staying sober if you struggle with addictions to alcohol and drugs in addition to nicotine. Addictive substances like drugs, cigarettes, and alcohol are intricately linked, as they use the same neuro-pathways in the brain. When one fires, it stimulates the demand

[16] For example, *Psychological Magazine* published a study from Washington University School of Medicine which showed that more people stayed alcohol free if they had also quit smoking.

for the other(s). For example, nicotine inhibits chromatin, a modifying enzyme which increases the addictive quality of cocaine.

Recovery from drug addiction and alcoholism needs to include recovery from smoking if it is to be most successful. It's as simple as that.

When AA (Alcoholics Anonymous) started in the 1930s the two founders, Bill W. and Dr. Bob, were smokers themselves and did not heed the advice of the Oxford Group in England (who helped develop the program) to get people to quit smoking at the same time as stopping drinking. Both men eventually died from smoking-related diseases, and thousands of AA members have ended up going the same way as a result.

The mortality rate associated with chronic cigarette smoking is four times greater than the mortality related to alcoholism. How sad to successfully give up alcohol to then die prematurely from cigarette addiction. My advice would be to get it all over and done with at the same time. The withdrawals won't be any worse, contrary to what anyone (usually another smoker with no intention of giving up) may tell you.

By the way, lobelia has been seen to help alcoholism too, so give it a try. You can buy the capsule version and use the powder in your cheek rather than the alcohol tincture version.

Five-minute contemplation: "Darkness is simply absence of light."

Chapter 28

Tips for Cleaning Out Your Lungs

"I draw sweet air / Deeply and long, / As pure as prayer, / As sweet as song. / Where lilies glow / And roses wreath, / Heart-joy I know / Is just to breathe." Robert William Service, "Breath Is Enough"

Now that you have stopped pumping toxic waste into yourself you may feel inspired to get your body back to health. There are a number of things you can do to clean out your body and repair some of the damage caused by smoking.

Soybeans: Consuming foods and drinks that contain soy may improve lung function and reduce shortness of breath. Besides being good for the lungs, soy also lowers cholesterol and treats symptoms of menopause. Just make sure it's not GMO, which is hard to do in the USA where 90% of soybeans are genetically modified. Soy is not good for people who are trying to avoid estrogen.

Lemon: Lemon and lime juice are very helpful for the quitting process as they alkalize the body and are also antibacterial, antiviral, and antioxidant.

Drink plenty of water: This will help to clean out toxins and nicotine that have accumulated in your lungs, and the rest of your body, after years of smoking.

Antioxidants: Broccoli, green tea, apples, and other fruits and vegetables rich in antioxidants can help repair and protect your lungs. One study[17] has shown that people who consume more than five apples a week have better lung function. Broccoli, Brussels sprouts, and cauliflower are also shown to lower the risk of lung cancer.

Omega-3: Foods rich in omega-3 such as fatty fish or flax can really help improve lung function even if you have Chronic Obstructive Pulmonary Disease (COPD). Omega-3 fatty acids decrease mucus production.

Mucus-producing foods: Stop eating mucus-producing foods such as sugar, artificial sweeteners, or refined flour and soft drinks, as well as products containing caffeine.

Breathing exercises: Relax and breathe deeply through your nose and exhale through your mouth for about 5-10 minutes every day.

Increase the capacity of lungs: Our life expectancy is directly dependent on the capacity of the lungs. If the lungs do not work optimally to supply oxygen throughout the body, then all metabolic processes are compromised. One effective way to increase your lung capacity is to play an instrument such as the saxophone, trumpet, or even the recorder. Practicing for 10-15 minutes a day will improve your lungs. If you are not musically inclined you can blow up balloons or buy a little lung-training gadget from the pharmacy that you blow into (one is called Expand-a-Lung) or just get outside, walk, and breathe deeply.

Five-minute contemplation: "The consciousness that created the universe dwells within me." (I am using this one again because it's so powerful.)

---

[17] Department of Public Health Sciences, St. George's Hospital Medical School, 1999.

Chapter 29

Staying Quit Forever and Ever

"We all listen to two voices. One voice leads us to our vices. The other voice leads us to our virtues. One voice brings evil. One voice brings good. The key is to listen to the right voice." Tom Krause

Staying quit is incredibly simple. Never have another puff.

It sounds easy enough right now. The trick, however, is actually to remember this in the future and not to fall into the trap of believing you could get away with having "just one." If I had a dollar for every time I've heard that from people who have relapsed I'd be a wealthy woman.

I know I said this before, but I want to say it again in case you did not really accept it the first time. Once you have been a smoker there is no "having just one." If you do, you will instantly be grabbed again by the nicotine demon. It sounds a bit dramatic and if you've not broken a period of being a non-smoker by supposedly having "just one," you will tend to think you know best when that moment of choice arises. I am telling you again. If you smoke a cigarette at any time in the future you will be back to smoking – as many as you ever did, or more – within a few days. Stay vigilant. Listen for that cunning voice and recognize it as not your own. If you get fooled, the bars will come down and you'll find yourself imprisoned once again.

There is no amount of stress or anger or sadness that warrants you becoming a smoker again. Someone will die and your brain will say you need to smoke. A relationship will end and a well-meaning friend will offer you a cigarette. You'll lose your job, be angry and hurt, and think about going to the store and buying a pack. A strong negative emotion will trigger the primitive survival part of your brain and attempt to override your intelligent cortex that knows you don't smoke. This ancient reptilian brain can only tell you what to do based on what it has done thousands and thousands of times in the past, back in the days when you were a smoker.

So, you'll smoke one and then what?

You may get ten minutes of relief, if you are lucky, and a bad taste in your mouth. But will the person not be dead? Will the relationship be good again? Will you miraculously get your job back?

No.

But you will be a smoker again: compounding the problems you already have. You'll also be less able to deal with those problems as the stress generated by smoking kicks back in. Not only that but you'll have a lot less money and a lower self-esteem.

All you need to do is remember "*I DON'T SMOKE NO MATTER WHAT.*" Walk away from whatever is happening and take 3-4 deep slow breaths. Endorphins will be released, your heart rate will go down, your blood pressure will return to normal, and the overwhelming emotion will become bearable once again. You will suddenly realize that smoking is the last thing in the world you need right now.

What about a New Year's Eve party? You get offered a big cigar – a really rare one from Cuba. You know, the "big shot" kind that says success and money. And because you've had a couple of drinks you think, *"Well, I haven't smoked for a whole year and this is a special occasion so I could have one, right? I mean* ***they*** *are all doing it."*

And guess what, Bam! You are back to square one. Within a couple of days you'll be smoking just as if you'd never stopped. That's a big price to pay for one cigar.

All you need to do is turn to the cigar giver and say, *"Please enjoy but I AM a non-smoker."* He or she may be one of those people able to smoke a cigar once in a blue moon but once you have been a habitual smoker this is no longer an option.

Never call the demon back

"It's the spark that ignites you, and the drive to keep going. It's the desire that burns, and a promise to keep fanning the flames." R.J. Reynolds, Tobacco Manufacturers

This last quote was taken from the back of a special edition of Camel Blue cigarettes. When I first saw it I was shocked. It was clearly a curse to send the smoker to hell, right there in full view, on the back of the pack.

On the front of the same pack was the word "Passion" written across a pair of filthy hands. The nails were black and broken – just as if the person had scraped their way out of a shallow grave. I know it sounds crazy but I have the pack here right beside me. I was amazed that R.J. Reynolds could be so up-front about their intent. Why not though? They know fear makes people want to smoke after all.

So be fearless and stay alert. Stay conscious of the black magic and send it back from whence it came. Never ignite that spark again, despite their evil wishes.

Think of it like this. You know those old movies where the vampire is "killed" in the 15th century, and he's buried deep in the earth in a coffin bound by thick chains. Then it flashes forward to the present and some construction-site worker unearths him. They open the coffin and they see him all shriveled and motionless and imagine him to be dead. Night falls and a little mouse walks next to the dried bony hand which…grabs the mouse and stuffs it into the vampire's mouth, where he sucks it dry. Once that little bit of blood enters his system the vampire opens his red eyes and is instantly restored. He jumps out of the coffin and he's hungry. I mean REALLY hungry. He looks around for a real meal. There is no stopping him now!

Well your little demon is just like that. You might think he's gone, you might think he's dead. But no, he's just asleep, waiting for the opportunity for that little puff that will bring him back to life, hungrier than ever!

And he's clever and he's patient. And when he whispers in your ear, know it's him talking, and not you. *You* don't smoke so whatever is suggested can't be true in any case.

And whenever you think about smoking (which you will now and then, and that's okay) just be thankful you don't actually have to do it anymore.

Earlier, when I said absolutely everyone starts smoking again if they have just one cigarette, it probably reminded you of someone who did have a puff once and managed to not start again. Of course only 90% of people start smoking again when they have one cigarette and you could be one of the lucky 10%. I'm a top 10% kind of person myself and I'm sure you are, too. But think of it this way. I have a gun with ten chambers into which I slide nine bullets. I spin the cylinder and hand it to you. We could put a large bet on it – a million dollars if you survive. Go on, you are a lucky person, a top 10% kind of person in fact, you go first!

Go on…hey, what's the problem?

I hope you get my point. Your life may depend upon on it.

Five-minute contemplation: "My soul's purpose on this Earth is to raise its vibration."

Chapter 30

A Demon or Just Uncle Bob?

"Soul attachment and release is a topic that is not discussed much. Yes it is real." Lawrence Wilson, M.D.

From my work as a hypnotist doing Spirit Release I thought I'd add this little story to these pages. The knowledge that this kind of thing exists might help someone with the same problem, and everyone else will probably find it fascinating.

On a number of occasions I have worked with people who have an addiction that they simply couldn't break no matter what they tried. Once in a hypnotic trance it would be revealed that a discarnate entity (a dead person's spirit) had attached itself to my client. This entity stayed within the energy-body of the live person and got *them* to do what *it* wanted to do. If it had been an alcoholic in life, it would get the person to drink. If it had been a heroin addict, it would get the person to take heroin. In this particular case "someone" was getting my client to smoke.

John (not his real name of course) came to see me for quitting smoking. No matter what he tried, he always ended up smoking. He told me it felt like he was being controlled by someone else. He did not even like smoking, but no sooner did he resolve not to smoke than he would find himself halfway back from the store with a cigarette in his hand. John was an oddity too, because after not smoking his entire youth he had suddenly taken up smoking two packs a day at the age of thirty-six, and had developed a nasty cough to go with it almost immediately.

I put him into a light trance which allowed him to enter his subconscious and to see within. *"I see Uncle Bob,"* he said. *"He's grinning and waving a cigarette at me!"*

It turns out that old Uncle Bob, a heavy smoker of 43 years, died of lung cancer around the time John turned thirty-six. Uncle Bob figured he'd have to give up smoking if he went to the Light so he decided to stay with his favorite nephew, John, and carry on as before.

Needless to say, I explained to Uncle Bob that he was having a disastrous effect on John's health, and persuaded him to go to the Light. His deceased wife came to meet him and he flicked the cigarette away before smiling and taking her hand.

John never picked up another cigarette and his cough immediately stopped.

If your instinct tells you something like this could be happening to you, please give me a call. I'd be delighted to help.

If you think this whole story sounds totally ridiculous, that's okay too. You can see it as just a powerful image that allows the subconscious to let go of the addiction.

Five-minute contemplation: "Consciousness is eternal."

Chapter 31

Breathe in the Love

"Using the power of your heart to balance thoughts and emotions, you can achieve energy, mental clarity – and feel better, fast, anywhere." Institute of HeartMath

I promised earlier on in the book to give you an additional breathing technique. This one was developed by an organization called the Institute of HeartMath, in order to help people overcome anger and anxiety issues. It is incredibly powerful.

Now that you are a non-smoker it is time to breathe fresh air as opposed to smoke. It is time to feel love as opposed to fear (fear is the opposite of love, not hate as you may think). It is time for you to increase your vibration from that of a nervous enslaved smoker to a free relaxed human being.

As I explained in the "Introduction to Tapping" chapter, emotions all have their own frequency. Fear, anger, and craving have a low vibration and love has a much higher vibration. When you choose to feel love, the lower vibrations are all transmuted to the point where you no longer feel them at all.

So this is how the process goes. After you've read through the exercise once, close your eyes and start the breathing-in through the nose, fill your lungs, hold for a few seconds, and then release slowly through pursed lips.

Now this time do the same thing but imagine the air is being inhaled into your heart and then exhaled from your solar plexus (your stomach area just below your diaphragm). Imagine it coming in like light or sparkling air. Do this a few times to practice the visualization.

Now just breathe normally and imagine what love feels like. If you can't feel love, go to a feeling of deep appreciation. Let this feeling fill your body. Perhaps you are looking at your newborn baby in your arms, the love of your life smiling at you, or your dog as he sleeps. Perhaps you are out on the water, on a mountain, a beach, or in a green meadow and you feel such appreciation for being alive. Notice how good it feels. Notice how it almost bubbles through your body. Allow yourself to really feel that love and deep appreciation. It makes you want to smile.

Now go back to breathing slowly and deeply into your heart, except that this time as you breathe in, you are going to imagine you are breathing in that feeling of love. Breathe that love into your heart, filling up your heart, filling up your chest with love.

The frequency of love or deep appreciation looks like a coherent sine wave – a smooth curved regular wave. As you breathe, take up the same rhythm: smooth and calm and regular.

Breathe the love into your heart and blow it out from your solar plexus. You can even imagine the exhaled breath like old gray smoke as it's blown out from your stomach.

Breathe like this perhaps ten times, keeping it really slow and smooth – the idea is not to hyperventilate. Then stop and notice how you feel, how calm you feel, how at peace you feel. Notice how that anger, anxiety, or craving has simply melted away.

Once you get good at it, start using this technique in everyday life. When a dangerous driver cuts you off on the freeway and you feel the anger start to rise, instead of shouting and making rude gestures and getting your knickers all in a twist (a great English saying that means raising your blood pressure!), simply inhale a feeling of love into your heart a couple of times. He'll drive on into his chaotic angry life and you will be back to enjoying the scenery and appreciating how great life is. Not only that, but your stress level will stay down and your immune system high. Meanwhile, the other driver will be well on the way to cancer of the spleen.

With the simple act of breathing we can become masters of our emotions. We no longer need be prey for craving, frustration, or anxiety, ever!

Five-minute contemplation: "My vibration endlessly ripples out across the entire universe."

Chapter 32

Contract Never to Sign

"Nothing in fine print is ever good news." Andy Rooney

Should you ever for some reason contemplate having that *one* cigarette, please read and sign the following small print in the contract first – just so you are clear what you are signing up for.

I do solemnly swear that I AGREE to:

1. enslave myself to cigarettes
2. be constantly stressed
3. be frequently miserable
4. massively increase my chance of getting cancer
5. increase the likelihood of having a heart attack or stroke
6. have less oxygen in my body
7. have less energy
8. have wrinkly grey skin
9. have smelly breath and hair
10. potentially lose my eyesight
11. have bad teeth and gums
12. be shunned socially

13. lose my natural ability to make dopamine and feel contentment
14. abuse my body with heavy metals, carcinogens, and tar
15. irradiate my body with polonium 210
16. waste hundreds or thousands of dollars per year that could otherwise be invested in vacations, education, or secure retirement
17. drain any savings my family or I have, in trying to save my life when I get sick from smoking
18. waste hours of every precious day smoking, thinking about smoking, and cleaning up after smoking
19. hang out by trash cans and on street corners
20. be less effective at work
21. feel guilty and have a reduced sense of my own self worth
22. be a horrible example to children
23. give thousands of dollars every year to the cigarette manufacturers so that they can live in luxury
24. reduce the length of my life by 10-15 years
25. invite the nicotine demon back into my life

I claim to be of sound mind and choose of my own free will to smoke.

Signed ______________________ Date________

Witness ___________________________

Chapter 33

I Salute You!

"I used to want the words 'She tried' on my tombstone. Now I want 'She did it.'" Katherine Dunham

Wow, you have made it to the end. You have read the whole book. That's great! I hope I have inspired you to quit smoking now and forever.

If you have just been reading and not actually taking any action yet, go back to Chapter 23, "The Day Before." Take one baby step at a time and you will succeed.

If this is it and the nicotine demon has been conquered: bravo! I am so proud of you, as you should be of yourself. This was no mean feat but you did it. You finally broke free. You are now well on the way to becoming the person that you should have been all along, before the interference of the nicotine demon!

I want to acknowledge you for your courage and your commitment. I wish you a wonderful, healthy, happy, and long life.

Just remember the No.1 rule of staying a non-smoker:

Non-smokers don't smoke!

Never have another puff, and you will stay free, forever and ever.

Amen.

Five-minute contemplation: “A sea of infinite potential radiates out from me.”

Appendix I

Instructions for Tapping

The basic form of Tapping that I now use is quite simple. It's just tapping specific points of the body in a certain order and then repeating it as the emotion or belief gets reduced and finally released.

One round of tapping consists of the setup and the tapping sequence.

The Setup

This is used to prepare and inform the energy body (and your powerful subconscious) what is to be worked on by acknowledging the problem.

You repeat the affirmation three times (out loud or in your head) while vigorously tapping on the "karate chop" point on one hand with the first three fingers of your other hand. This is in the middle of the fleshy part of the side of your hand below your little finger. Either hand will do.

The affirmation goes like this: "*Even though I have this ______________, I completely love and accept myself.*"

The issue could be this fear of flying, this anger at my father, pain in my knee, craving for chocolate, anxiety about my test, horror at what I saw, sadness about losing my boyfriend, shame at what they did to me, guilt for what I did, craving for a cigarette, belief that I can't stop smoking, etc.

To get as clear a description of the emotion as possible, close your eyes and feel where it is located in your body. Notice if it has a color, whether it's hard or soft, liquid or solid, heavy or light, if it's hot or cold, what it's made of, what shape it is, how large it is, etc.

For example: *"Even though I have this tight rubber ball of black anxiety trapped in my stomach at the thought of never having another cigarette, I completely love and accept myself."*

It does not matter if you believe the positive affirmation or not, just say it. If you really can't say the part about loving and accepting yourself, say, *"I'm okay."*

The Tapping Sequence

You tap on each point about seven to nine times using the pad of your middle finger (just beneath the nail). It does not matter which hand you use or which side of your body you tap on. In fact you can alternate. As you tap you say the reminder phrase or phrases which I'll cover in a moment.

Each energy meridian has two but we just tap on one end. The tapping locations are as follows.

- At the top of the head, on the crown
- At the beginning of the eyebrow, just above and to one side of the nose
- On the bone bordering the outside of the eye
- On the bone under the eye below the pupil
- Under your nose (closer to your nose than your lip)

- In the dip in the middle of your chin

- The junction where the sternum, collarbone, and first rib meet (one inch down and out from the U-shaped notch)

- On the side of the torso level with the nipple, about four inches below the armpit

- For men, one inch below the nipple; for ladies, where the underskin of the breast meets the chest wall

The Reminder Phrase(s)

The reminder phrase is used to tune into the problem. It is a short phrase that you say out loud each time you tap on a meridian point. You can start off with the issue as stated in the setup, like *"this anger at my father,"* and then it can change to *"this anger," "I am angry," "he made me feel angry,"* etc.

Try to make the description of the emotion as specific as possible. For instance: *"these hot red coals of anger trapped in my belly"* or *"this gray elastic band of anxiety stuck tight around my chest."*

At the end of each round take a deep breath.

Adjusting for the next round

Once you have completed a few rounds, close your eyes, go back to the issue in your mind, and assess the level of emotion or level of belief on a scale of one to ten (where ten is very intense and zero is nothing at all).

As the intensity goes down the setup affirmation needs to change. For example: *"Even though I still have this remaining light red rubber ball of anxiety at the thought of quitting smoking, I completely love and accept myself"* and the reminder phrase will be *"remaining anxiety."* The mind is literal and needs to know you are working on the remainder of the problem.

Allowing the body to release the emotion

Once the intensity of an emotion has been lowered down to three or less, start changing the reminder phrase to allow release. For example: *"I allow this (anger) to be released....I allow my chest to release this anger....I allow my body to release this anger....I allow every cell in my body to release this anger right now."*

Ending on a positive

When you feel the emotion has all but disappeared, add some positive affirmations as you tap. For example: *"I allow all the spaces where the (anxiety) was to be filled with the white light of love....I feel compassion in my heart....I feel forgiveness in my chest...It feels so good to have finally let this last remaining fear go...the last of this worry....all filled with light....my heart is filled with the light of love and compassion, etc."*

What can I use Tapping for?

You can use Tapping for anything. There are no negative effects. It can be used for all kinds of first aid, pain, and inflammation including burns, cuts, bleeding, bee stings, bites, allergies, rashes, muscle pain, swelling, chronic pain, and sore throats. It can be used for colds, flu symptoms, aches, headaches, backache, neck pain, toothache, and all manner of disease stemming from trapped negative emotion.

Tapping is an incredibly fast and effective way to release negative emotions: shame, humiliation, guilt, unworthiness, blame, grief, regret, fear, anxiety, craving, greed, anger, hate, pride, or scorn.

Tapping can also be used to let go of unhelpful beliefs about money, addiction, relationships, health, life and death, etc. For instance: *"Even though I've failed before and I feel I'll fail again, I completely love and accept myself."*

If you have any questions about using Tapping or would like to have a personal session with me then please email me at helenhypnotist@gmail.com or go to my business website, www.helenbasinger.com.

Appendix II

EFT for Fear of Quitting

Most people when they decide to quit feel a certain amount of anxiety about doing it. It could be fear of the withdrawal symptoms, fear of feeling overwhelmed with stress, or fear of failing.

You can follow the EFT sequence below by having a friend read it to you or you can go onto the website www.quitsmokingnowandforever.com and follow along with me.

The Sequence

Tapping on the side of the hand: *Even though I'm scared of giving up cigarettes, I completely love and accept myself*

Even though I'm secretly terrified of what will happen if I no longer smoke, I completely love and accept myself

Even though I have this tension in my head, tightness in my belly, and pressure in my head from the stress of thinking about quitting smoking forever, I completely love and accept myself

- Head: *This fear I have of not smoking that's trapped in my body, in my* ________ (wherever you feel that fear in your body)
- Eyebrow: *I'm scared something bad will happen if I quit*
- Side of eye: *I'm fearful of not having cigarettes as a crutch*

- Under eye: *This fear of not breathing in those 7,000 chemicals anymore*
- Under nose: *I'm scared of not being able to suck that gray smoke into my lungs every hour or so*
- Chin: *This terror I feel at the thought of not having my little friend, the cigarette, in my life*
- Collarbone: *I feel stressed at the thought of being healthy and normal again*
- Under arm: *This anxiety I feel at throwing my cigarettes away for good*
- Under breast: *This fear that has collected in me from all those cigarettes*
- Head: *It would be so good to let this fear of quitting go*
- Eyebrow: *I allow my body to start to release this anxiety that I feel about quitting*
- Side of eye: *I allow this tight fear of not breathing in toxic smoke anymore to be released from my chest*
- Under eye: *I allow this squeezing anxiety of not having cigarettes in my life to be released from my belly*
- Under nose: *I allow this fear of being natural and normal again to leave my head*
- Collarbone: *It's been so long I hardly remember what it feels like to be natural and normal – I let this fear of that go, right now*
- Under arm: *Allowing this fear of what I will do with all those thousands of extra dollars each year to leave my body*
- Under breast: *Allowing this fear of having 10-15 extra years of life to leave my mind*

- Head: *I allow my hands to release this anxiety about not holding a cigarette*
- Eyebrow: *I allow my lips to release this fear of no longer sucking on a cigarette*
- Side of eye: *I allow the back of my throat to release this fear of no longer breathing in thick toxic fumes from a cigarette*
- Under eye: *I allow my lungs to release this fear of no longer being damaged and covered in tar*
- Under nose: *I allow my chest to release this fear of having full oxygen and being free from nicotine right now*
- Collarbone: *I allow every cell in my body to release this anxiety and stress about becoming a non-smoker right now*
- Under arm: *Releasing this fear of no longer puffing on dead tobacco leaves and 600 additives*
- Under breast: *I allow this dark fear to be released from my blood*
- Head: *I allow the light of courage to enter the space where all this dark fear of quitting used to be*
- Eyebrow: *I allow this light of love and courage to fill up all the space where the fear used to be*
- Side of eye: *Releasing this last bit of fear of being free*
- Under eye: *Releasing this last bit of tension in my belly*
- Collarbone: *Allowing my chest to release this last tight stress and apprehension*
- Under arm: *Releasing this last bit of fear from my brain*
- Under breast: *Remembering that no one ever died of a craving, no one went mad from a craving, allowing this courage to fill my heart*
- Head: *Allowing this bright white light of courage to fill up all the space where that anxiety used to be*

- Take a deep breath.

Close your eyes and imagine not having any cigarettes in your pocket, purse, or even close by. Imagine going through an entire day with no cigarettes at all. On a scale of one to ten how nervous do you still feel?

Repeat the process until you have reduced your fear down to nothing – until you start to feel courage and optimism.

Appendix III

Tapping for Craving

Before you begin, close your eyes, and imagine you have not had a cigarette for a few hours. Where do you feel that craving and desire in your body? What color does it have? Is it stuck in that part of your body, pressing down onto that part of your body, or squeezing around that part of your body? What would it be made out of? How heavy is it? Now begin the process.

Once again you can find this Tapping session on the website www.quitsmokingnowandforever.com or you can simply read it and follow the tapping sequence yourself.

Tapping on the side of the hand (karate chop point):

- *Even though I crave cigarettes, I completely love and forgive myself*
- *Even though I have this strong craving for nicotine, that seems stronger than me, I completely love and accept who I am anyway*
- *Even though I have this craving like a ________________ in (on or around) my ______________, I completely love and accept myself*
- Top of head: *I crave cigarettes*
- Eyebrow: *I need to smoke cigarettes*

- Side of eye: *I have this deep urge to smoke*
- Under eye: *My throat wants to suck in that smoke*
- Under nose: *My lungs want to breathe in that smoke*
- Chin: *My brain cries out for nicotine like a baby needing to be fed*
- Collarbone: *I feel this craving in my _____________, like a _____________*
- Under arm: *This craving needs to be fulfilled*
- Under breast: *This craving in my head*
- Top of head: *This craving in my chest*
- Side of eye: *This desire to pick up a cigarette*
- Under eye: *This craving that runs my life*
- Under nose: *This craving that controls me*
- Chin: *It would be so good to let this craving go*
- Collarbone: *What would it be like to let this craving go?*
- Under arm: *How would it feel to not need to smoke?*
- Under breast: *Would it be okay not to want one?*
- Top of head: *I allow this craving to be released from my mind*
- Eyebrow: *I allow this craving to be released from my brain*
- Side of eye: *I allow this craving to be released from my throat*
- Under eye: *I allow this desire to be released from my lips*
- Under nose: *I allow my lungs to release this craving to smoke*
- Chin: *I allow my muscles to release this craving for nicotine*
- Collarbone: *I allow this craving to be released from my blood*
- Under arm: *I allow this craving to be released from my arms and legs*
- Under breast: *I allow this craving to be released from every cell in my body*

- Top of head*: I see this ________________ in (on or around) my ______________getting smaller and smaller*
- Eyebrow*: I allow this ___________ to get looser and looser*
- Side of eye: *I allow this ______________ to get lighter and lighter*
- Under eye*: I allow this __________________ to get softer and softer*
- Under nose: *Releasing this ______________from my ___________*
- Chin*: I allow my ____________ to release this craving*
- Collarbone: *I allow this craving to get smaller and smaller, lighter and lighter*
- Under arm: *Seeing this __________________ melting away*
- Under breast: *Washing away this craving from my body completely*
- Top of head: *It's okay if I don't want to smoke*
- Eyebrow: *It's okay to choose not to smoke anymore*
- Side of eye: *It's okay to let this craving go*
- Under eye*: I allow this desire to harm myself with cigarettes to be released*
- Under nose: *I allow this craving to be released from my mind*
- Chin: *I allow this craving to be replaced with a desire to be healthy*
- Collarbone*: I allow this craving for nicotine to be replaced with a desire to be free for the rest of my life*
- Under arm: *Allowing this bizarre craving to suck toxic chemicals into my body to be released right now*
- Under breast: *Allowing myself to love my self*
- Top of head: *Allowing myself to no longer be at the mercy of this manufactured craving*
- Eyebrow: *Allowing this craving to leave my body completely*
- Side of eye: *Allowing this craving to be a thing of the past*
- Under eye: *Allowing myself to walk on and leave it behind*

- Under nose: *Allowing this craving to get smaller and smaller, weaker and weaker, looser and looser, less and less heavy*
- Chin: *Allowing this desire to smoke to be washed clean from my body*
- Collarbone: *Allowing myself to be washed clean*
- Under arm: *Allowing all the space where the craving used to be to be filled with peace*
- Under breast: *Allowing every cell in my body to be filled with love*
- Top of head: *I allow this craving to be replaced with a beautiful bright light of love and joy right now*
- Take a deep breath.

Think about craving. How much would you like to smoke a cigarette right now? How about in a couple of hours? Where would it be on a scale one to ten?

Do the sequence again and again until you no longer have any desire to smoke.

Appendix IV

Tapping for People Who 'Love' to Smoke

Some people, despite wanting to quit and knowing how bad smoking is for them, still experience a lingering fondness for cigarettes. The following sequence will help to release that artificially created pleasure.

You can follow along with it here:

www.quitsmokingnowandforever.com.

Tapping on the side of the hand.

Even though I want to quit but there's a part of me that still loves to smoke, I completely love and forgive myself

Even though I really enjoy sucking in toxic smoke, I love the smell and the taste, I completely love and accept who I am anyway

Even though I enjoy smoking socially and taking my little cigarette breaks, I completely love and accept myself

- Top of head: *Part of me loves to smoke*
- Eyebrow: *I love smoking*
- Side of eye: *I love smoking my cigarettes*
- Under eye: *It feels rebellious and exciting to smoke*

- Under nose: *I love the taste of smoke*
- Chin*: I love to feel the smoke going down into my lungs*
- Collarbone*: I love the way the cigarette feels between my fingers*
- Under arm: *It feels deliciously naughty to smoke*
- Under breast: *Smoking is such fun*
- Top of head: *It's hard to imagine not liking it*
- Side of eye*: I really enjoy sucking that thick smoke into my lungs*
- Under eye: *I like to smoke with my smoker friends*
- Under nose*: I love sucking on a cigarette out by the trash cans*
- Chin: *Part of me really enjoys playing with fire*
- Collarbone*: I love breathing out great plumes of smoke*
- Under arm: *I love the way my teeth and fingers get stained*
- Under breast: *I love the way my clothes, breath, and hair smell*
- Top of head: *Really, part of me enjoys it when 200 neuro-chemicals mess with my head*
- Eyebrow: *I enjoy knowing that over 250 carcinogens and poisons are entering my body with every puff*
- Side of eye: *I love the thought that my hard earned money is going to make the cigarette manufacturers richer and richer instead of going to my family or me*
- Under eye: *There is a part of me that still enjoys being chained to smoking*
- Under nose: *There is a part of me however that longs to be free*
- Chin: *There is a part of me that wants to die a young and miserable death*
- Collarbone*: Even though the soul in me wants to live and be healthy*
- Under arm: *I like to take time out to smoke*

- Under breast: *Could I be allowed to just take time out to be and breathe fresh air?*
- Top of head: *I allow this belief that I like smoking to leave my mind*
- Eyebrow: *I allow myself to see that smoking keeps me trapped, just relieving me for a few short minutes before it starts to wear off*
- Side of eye: *I allow myself to see I've been caught like a rat in a wheel*
- Under eye: *I allow myself to really recognize what cigarettes taste like*
- Under nose: *I allow myself to really smell again what cigarettes smell like*
- Chin: *I allow myself to release years of clever programming, releasing the Marlboro Man and the seductive elegant smoking ladies*
- Collarbone: *Releasing that belief that I've been choosing to smoke, as I see now how I have been tricked and duped all along*
- Under arm: *Releasing this belief that I actually like breathing in addictive toxic fumes*
- Under breast: *Releasing this belief that I like paying someone to kill me slowly*
- Top of head: *I allow this belief that I actually enjoy nicotine slavery to be released from my body and mind right now*
- Eyebrow: *I allow this desire to smoke to be replaced by a desire to be free, happy, and healthy*
- Side of eye: *I allow this belief that smoking is fun to be released from my conscious and subconscious mind*
- Under eye: *I allow this desire to smoke to be released from every cell in my body right now*

- Under nose: *I allow this belief, that I am actually giving up something, to be released*
- Chin: *I allow myself to embrace a new me that enjoys health and well-being*
- Collarbone: *I allow this desire to smoke a cigarette to fall away*
- Under arm*: I allow myself to see cigarettes for what they truly are – corruption, greed, disease, addiction, and death*
- Under breast: *I allow it to be okay for me not to like it anymore and I allow myself to be free*
- Top of head: *I allow this addiction to be replaced with a beautiful bright light of love and joy right now*
- Take a deep breath.

Think about your love of smoking. Where would it be on a scale of one to ten?

Do the sequence again and again until you no longer think you enjoy smoking.

Appendix V

Additives in Cigarettes – Maximizing the Addictive Effect

Following is a list of all 599 things that the cigarette manufacturers add to tobacco to make you as addicted as they possibly can.

Earlier in the book I covered the fact that the addition of menthol, acetaldehyde, and ammonia is the main culprit for making cigarettes the most addictive drug on the planet. As you look through the rest of the list you will see lots of hard to pronounce names of chemicals. Many of these add to the speed and amount of nicotine that is delivered to the brain; others numb the body from noticing the damage that's being done.

I decided to include the whole list because when you see it you'll understand the full scale of the cigarette makers' deviousness. Nothing has been left out of the equation: no legal stimulant, flavor, chemical, or essential oil. They are increasing the pleasure you feel from smoking by adding our favorite things: coffee, tea, chocolate, hops, wine, cinnamon, rum, rose essence, apple juice, etc. No doubt it works the other way around too, so that any time you taste or smell any of these things you are programmed to want to light up.

In an age where every food has a list of its ingredients and calorie content so that we know the exact components used to make our peanut butter or our packets of macaroni cheese, ask yourself where the list of added ingredients is on the cigarette pack that slyly proclaims itself as simply "smooth golden Virginia tobacco."

A

Acetanisole

Acetic acid

Acetoin

Acetophenone

6-Acetoxydihydrotheaspirane

2-Acetyl-3-Ethylpyrazine

2-Acetyl-5-Methylfuran

Acetylpyrazine

2-Acetylpyridine

3-Acetylpyridine

2-Acetylthiazole

Aconitic Acid

dl-Alanine

Alfalfa Extract

Allspice Extract, Oleoresin, and Oil

Allyl Hexanoate

Allyl Ionone

Almond Bitter Oil

Ambergris Tincture

Ammonia

Ammonium Bicarbonate

Ammonium Hydroxide

Ammonium sulfide

Amyl Alcohol

Amyl Butyrate

Amyl Formate

Amyl Octanoate

alpha-Amylcinnamaldehyde

Amyris Oil

trans-Anethole

Angelica Root Extract, Oil and Seed Oil

Anise

Anise Star, Extract and Oils

Anisyl Acetate

Anisyl Alcohol

Anisyl Formate

Anisyl Phenylacetate

Apple Juice Concentrate, Extract, and Skins

Apricot Extract and Juice Concentrate

L-Arginine

Asafetida Fluid Extract and Oil

Ascorbic Acid

L-Asparagine Monohydrate

L-Aspartic Acid

B

Balsam Peru and Oil

Basil Oil

Bay leaf, Oil and Sweet Oil

Beeswax White

Beet Juice Concentrate

Benzaldehyde

Benzaldehyde Glyceryl Acetal

Benzoic acid, Benzoin

Benzoin Resin

Benzophenone

Benzyl Alcohol

Benzyl Benzoate

Benzyl Butyrate

Benzyl Cinnamate

Benzyl Propionate

Benzyl salicylate

Bergamot Oil

Bisabolene

Black Currant Buds Absolute

Borneol

Bornyl Acetate

Buchu Leaf Oil

1,3-Butanediol

2,3-Butanedione

1-Butanol

2-Butanone

4(2-Butenylidene)-3,5,5-Trimethyl-2-Cyclohexen-1-One

Butter, Butter Esters, and Butter Oil

Butyl acetate

Butyl butyrate

Butyl butyryl lactate

Butyl isovalerate

Butyl phenylacetate

Butyl ndecylenate

3-Butylidenephthalide

Butyric Acid

C

Cadinene

Caffeine

Calcium Carbonate

Camphene

Cananga Oil

Capsicum Oleoresin

Caramel color

Caraway Oil

Carbon Dioxide

Cardamom Oleoresin, Extract, Seed Oil, and Powder

Carob Bean and Extract

beta-Carotene

Carrot Oil

Carvacrol

4-Carvomenthenol

L-Carvone

beta-Caryophyllene

beta-Caryophyllene Oxide

Cascarilla Oil and Bark Extract

Cassia Bark Oil

Cassie Absolute and Oil

Castoreum Extract, Tincture and Absolute

Cedar Leaf Oil

Cedarwood Oil Terpenes and Virginiana

Cedrol

Celery Seed Extract, Solid, Oil, And Oleoresin

Cellulose Fiber

Chamomile Flower Oil And Extract

Chicory Extract

Chocolate

Cinnamaldehyde

Cinnamic Acid

Cinnamon Leaf Oil, Bark Oil, and Extract

Cinnamyl Acetate

Cinnamyl Alcohol

Cinnamyl Cinnamate

Cinnamyl Isovalerate

Cinnamyl Propionate

Citral

Citric Acid

Citronella Oil

dl-Citronellol

Citronellyl Butyrate

Citronellyl Isobutyrate

Civet Absolute

Clary Oil

Clover Tops, Red Solid Extract

Cocoa

Cocoa Shells, Extract, Distillate And Powder

Coconut Oil

Coffee

Cognac White and Green Oil

Copaiba Oil

Coriander Extract and Oil

Corn Oil

Corn Silk

Costus Root Oil

Cubeb Oil

Cuminaldehyde

para-Cymene

L-Cysteine

D

Dandelion Root Solid Extract

Davana Oil

2-trans,4-trans-Decadienal

delta-Decalactone

gamma-Decalactone

Decanal

Decanoic acid

1-Decanol

2-Decenal

Dehydromenthofurolactone

Diammonium phosphate

Diethyl Malonate

Diethyl Sebacate

2,3-Diethylpyrazine

Dihydro Anethole

5,7-Dihydro-2-Methylthieno(3,4-D) Pyrimidine

Dill Seed Oil and Extract

meta-Dimethoxybenzene

para-Dimethoxybenzene

2,6-Dimethoxyphenol

Dimethyl Succinate

3,4-Dimethyl-1,2-Cyclopentanedione

3,5-Dimethyl-1,2-Cyclopentanedione

3,7-Dimethyl-1,3,6-Octatriene

4,5-Dimethyl-3-Hydroxy-2,5-Dihydrofuran-2-One

6,10-Dimethyl-5,9-Undecadien-2-One

3,7-Dimethyl-6-Octenoic Acid

2,4 Dimethylacetophenone

alpha,para-Dimethylbenzyl Alcohol

alpha,alpha-Dimethylphenethyl Acetate

alpha,alpha Dimethylphenethyl Butyrate

2,3-Dimethylpyrazine

2,5-Dimethylpyrazine

2,6-Dimethylpyrazine

Dimethyltetrahydrobenzofuranone

delta-Dodecalactone

gamma-Dodecalactone

E

para-Ethoxybenzaldehyde

Ethyl 10-Undecenoate

Ethyl 2-Methylbutyrate

Ethyl acetate

Ethyl acetoacetate

Ethyl alcohol

Ethyl benzoate

Ethyl butyrate

Ethyl cinnamate

Ethyl decanoate

Ethyl fenchol

Ethyl furoate

Ethyl heptanoate

Ethyl hexanoate

Ethyl isovalerate

Ethyl lactate

Ethyl laurate

Ethyl levulinate

Ethyl maltol

Ethyl methylphenylglycidate

Ethyl myristate

Ethyl nonanoate

Ethyl octadecanoate

Ethyl octanoate

Ethyl oleate

Ethyl palmitate

Ethyl phenylacetate

Ethyl propionate

Ethyl salicylate

Ethyl trans-2-butenoate

Ethyl valerate

Ethyl vanillin

2-Ethyl (or Methyl)-(3,5 and 6)-Methoxypyrazine

2-Ethyl-1-Hexanol,3-Ethyl-2-Hydroxy-2-Cyclopenten-1-One

2-Ethyl-3,(5 or 6)-Dimethylpyrazine

5-Ethyl-3-Hydroxy-4-Methyl-2(5H)-Furanone

2-Ethyl-3-Methylpyrazine

3-Ethylpyridine

4-Ethylbenzaldehyde

4-Ethylguaiacol

4-Ethylphenol (para-Ethylphenol)

Eucalyptol

F

Farnesol

D-Fenchone

Fennel Sweet Oil

Fenugreek, Extract, Resin, and Absolute

fig Juice Concentrate

Food Starch Modified

Furfuryl Mercaptan

4-(2-Furyl)-3-Buten-2-One

G

Galbanum Oil

Genet Absolute

Gentian Root Extract

Geraniol

Geranium Rose Oil

Geranyl Acetate

Geranyl Butyrate

Geranyl Formate

Geranyl Isovalerate

Geranyl Phenylacetate

Ginger Oil and Oleoresin

L-Glutamic Acid

L-Glutamine

Glycerol

Glycyrrhizin Ammoniated

Grape Juice Concentrate

Guaiac Wood Oil

Guaiacol

Guar Gum

H

2,4-Heptadienal

gamma-Heptalactone

Heptanoic Acid

2-Heptanone

3-Hepten-2-One

2-Hepten-4-One

4-Heptenal

trans-2-Heptenal

Heptyl acetate

omega-6-Hexadecenlactone

gamma-Hexalactone

Hexanal

Hexanoic acid

2-Hexen-1-Ol

3-Hexen-1-Ol

cis-3-Hexen-1-Yl Acetate

2-Hexenal

3-Hexenoic Acid

trans-2-Hexenoic Acid

cis-3-Hexenyl Formate

Hexyl 2-Methylbutyrate

Hexyl Acetate

Hexyl Alcohol

Hexyl Phenylacetate

L-Histidine

Honey

Hops Oil

Hydrolyzed Milk Solids

Hydrolyzed Plant Proteins

5-Hydroxy-2,4-Decadienoic Acid delta- Lactone

4-Hydroxy-2,5-Dimethyl-3(2H)-Furanone

2-Hydroxy-3,5,5-Trimethyl-2-Cyclohexen-1-One

4-Hydroxy -3-Pentenoic Acid Lactone

2-Hydroxy-4-Methylbenzaldehyde

4-Hydroxybutanoic Acid Lactone

Hydroxycitronellal

6-Hydroxydihydrotheaspirane

4-(para-Hydroxyphenyl)-2-Butanone

Hyssop Oil

I

Immortelle Absolute and Extract

alpha-Ionone

beta-Ionone

alpha-Irone

Isoamyl Acetate

Isoamyl Benzoate

Isoamyl Butyrate

Isoamyl Cinnamate

Isoamyl Formate, Isoamyl Hexanoate

Isoamyl Isovalerate

Isoamyl Octanoate

Isoamyl Phenylacetate

Isobornyl Acetate

Isobutyl Acetate

Isobutyl Alcohol

Isobutyl Cinnamate

Isobutyl Phenylacetate

Isobutyl Salicylate

2-Isobutyl-3-Methoxypyrazine

alpha-Isobutylphenethyl Alcohol

Isobutyraldehyde

Isobutyric Acid

d,l-Isoleucine

alpha-Isomethylionone

2-Isopropylphenol

Isovaleric Acid

J

Jasmine Absolute, Concrete and Oil

K

Kola Nut Extract

L

Labdanum Absolute and Oleoresin

Lactic Acid

Lauric Acid

Lauric Aldehyde

Lavandin Oil

Lavender oil

Lemon Oil and Extract

Lemongrass Oil

L-Leucine

Levulinic acid

Liquorice root, fluid, extract and powder

Lime Oil

Linalool

Linalool Oxide

Linalyl acetate

Linden Flowers

Lovage Oil And Extract

L-Lysine

M

Mace Powder, Extract and Oil

Magnesium Carbonate

Malic Acid

Malt and Malt Extract

Maltodextrin

Maltol

Maltyl Isobutyrate

Mandarin Oil

Maple Syrup and Concentrate

Mate Leaf, Absolute and Oil

para-Mentha-8-Thiol-3-One

Menthol

Menthone

Menthyl Acetate

dl-Methionine

Methoprene

2-Methoxy-4-Methylphenol

2-Methoxy-4-Vinylphenol

para-Methoxybenzaldehyde

1-(para-Methoxyphenyl)-1-Penten-3-One

4-(para-Methoxyphenyl)-2-Butanone

1-(para-Methoxyphenyl)-2-Propanone

Methoxypyrazine

Methyl 2-Furoate

Methyl 2-Octynoate

Methyl 2-Pyrrolyl Ketone

Methyl Anisate

Methyl anthranilate

Methyl Benzoate

Methyl Cinnamate

Methyl Dihydrojasmonate

Methyl Ester of Rosin, Partially Hydrogenated

Methyl Isovalerate

Methyl Linoleate (48%)

Methyl Linolenate (52%) Mixture

Methyl Naphthyl Ketone

Methyl Nicotinate

Methyl phenylacetate

Methyl Salicylate

Methyl Sulfide

3-Methyl-1-Cyclopentadecanone

4-Methyl-1-Phenyl-2-Pentanone

5-Methyl-2-Phenyl-2-Hexenal

5-Methyl-2-Thiophenecarboxaldehyde

6-Methyl-3,-5-Heptadien-2-One

2-Methyl-3-(para-Isopropylphenyl) Propionaldehyde

5-Methyl-3-Hexen-2-One

1-Methyl-3-Methoxy-4-Isopropylbenzene

4-Methyl-3-Pentene-2-One

2-Methyl-4-Phenylbutyraldehyde

6-Methyl-5-Hepten-2-One

4-Methyl-5-Thiazoleethanol

4-Methyl-5-Vinylthiazole

Methyl-alpha-Ionone

Methyl-trans-2-Butenoic Acid

4-Methylacetophenone

para-Methylanisole

alpha-Methylbenzyl Acetate

alpha-Methylbenzyl Alcohol

2-Methylbutyraldehyde

3-Methylbutyraldehyde

2-Methylbutyric Acid

alpha-Methylcinnamaldehyde

Methylcyclopentenolone

2-Methylheptanoic Acid

2-Methylhexanoic Acid

3-Methylpentanoic Acid

4-Methylpentanoic Acid

2-Methylpyrazine

5-Methylquinoxaline

2-Methyltetrahydrofuran-3-One

(Methylthio)Methylpyrazine (Mixture Of Isomers)

3-Methylthiopropionaldehyde

Methyl 3-Methylthiopropionate

2-Methylvaleric Acid

Mimosa Absolute and Extract

Molasses Extract and Tincture

Mountain Maple Solid Extract

Mullein Flowers

Myristaldehyde

Myristic acid

Myrrh Oil

N

beta-Napthyl Ethyl Ether

Nerol

Neroli Bigarde Oil

Nerolidol

Nona-2-trans,6-cis-dienal

2,6-Nonadien-1-ol

gamma-Nonalactone

Nonanal

Nonanoic Acid

Nonanone

trans-2-Nonen-1-ol

2-Nonenal

Nonyl Acetate

Nutmeg Powder and Oil

Nicotine

O

Oak chips extract and oil

Oakmoss absolute

9,12-Octadecadienoic acid (48%) and 9,12,15-Octadecatrienoic acid (52%)

delta-Octalactone

gamma-Octalactone

Octanal

Octanoic acid

1-Octanol

2-Octanone

3-Octen-2-one

1-Octen-3-ol

1-Octen-3-yl acetate

2-Octenal

Octyl isobutyrate

Oleic acid

Olibanum oil

Opoponax oil and gum

Orange blossom water, absolute, and leaf absolute

Orange oil and extract

Origanum oil

Orris concrete oil and root extract

P

Palmarosa Oil

Palmitic acid

Parsley Seed Oil

Patchouli Oil

omega-Pentadecalactone

2,3-Pentanedione

2-Pentanone

4-Pentenoic Acid

2-Pentylpyridine

Pepper Oil, Black And White

Peppermint Oil

Peruvian (Bois De Rose) Oil

Petitgrain Absolute, Mandarin Oil and Terpeneless Oil

alpha-Phellandrene

2-Phenenthyl Acetate

Phenethyl alcohol

Phenethyl Butyrate

Phenethyl Cinnamate

Phenethyl Isobutyrate

Phenethyl Isovalerate

Phenethyl Phenylacetate

Phenethyl Salicylate

1-Phenyl-1-Propanol

3-Phenyl-1-Propanol

2-Phenyl-2-Butenal

4-Phenyl-3-Buten-2-Ol

4-Phenyl-3-Buten-2-One

Phenylacetaldehyde

Phenylacetic Acid

L-Phenylalanine

3-Phenylpropionaldehyde

3-Phenylpropionic Acid

3-Phenylpropyl Acetate

3-Phenylpropyl Cinnamate

2-(3-Phenylpropyl)Tetrahydrofuran

Phosphoric Acid

Pimenta Leaf Oil

Pine Needle Oil, Pine Oil, Scotch

Pineapple Juice Concentrate

alpha-Pinene, beta-Pinene

D-Piperitone

Piperonal

Pipsissewa Leaf Extract

Plum Juice

Potassium Sorbate

L-Proline

Propenylguaethol

Propionic Acid

Propyl Acetate

Propyl para-Hydroxybenzoate

Propylene Glycol

3-Propylidenephthalide

Prune Juice and Concentrate

Pyridine

Pyroligneous Acid And Extract

Pyrrole

Pyruvic Acid

R

Raisin Juice Concentrate

Rhodinol

Rose Absolute and Oil

Rosemary Oil

Rum

Rum Ether

Rye Extract

S

Sage, Sage oil, and Sage oleoresin

Salicylaldehyde

Sandalwood oil, yellow

Sclareolide

Skatole

Smoke flavor

Snakeroot oil

Sodium acetate

Sodium benzoate

Sodium bicarbonate

Sodium carbonate

Sodium chloride

Sodium citrate

Sodium hydroxide

Solanone

Spearmint oil

Styrax extract, gum and oil

Sucrose octaacetate

Sugar alcohols

Sugars

T

Tagetes Oil
Tannic Acid
Tartaric Acid
Tea Leaf and Absolute
alpha-Terpineol
Terpinolene
Terpinyl Acetate
5,6,7,8-Tetrahydroquinoxaline
1,5,5,9-Tetramethyl-13-Oxatricyclo(8.3.0.0(4,9))Tridecane
2,3,4,5, and 3,4,5,6-Tetramethylethyl-Cyclohexanone
2,3,5,6-Tetramethylpyrazine
Thiamine Hydrochloride
Thiazole
L-Threonine
Thyme Oil, White and Red
Thymol
Tobacco Extracts
Tocopherols (mixed)
Tolu balsam Gum and Extract
Tolualdehydes
para-Tolyl 3-Methylbutyrate
para-Tolyl Acetaldehyde
para-Tolyl Acetate
para-Tolyl Isobutyrate
para-Tolyl Phenylacetate
Triacetin
2-Tridecanone
2-Tridecenal

Triethyl Citrate

3,5,5-Trimethyl-1-Hexanol

para,alpha,alpha-Trimethylbenzyl Alcohol

4-(2,6,6-Trimethylcyclohex-1-Enyl)But-2-En-4-One

2,6,6-Trimethylcyclohex-2-Ene-1,4-Dione

2,6,6-Trimethylcyclohexa-1,3-Dienyl Methan

4-(2,6,6-Trimethylcyclohexa-1,3-Dienyl)But-2-En-4-One

2,2,6-Trimethylcyclohexanone

2,3,5-Trimethylpyrazine

L-Tyrosine

U

delta-Undecalactone

gamma-Undecalactone

Undecanal

2-Undecanone

10-Undecenal

Urea

V

Valencene

Valeraldehyde

Valerian Root Extract, Oil and Powder

Valeric acid

gamma-Valerolactone

Valine

Vanilla Extract And Oleoresin

Vanillin

Veratraldehyde

Vetiver Oil

Vinegar

Violet Leaf Absolute

W

Walnut Hull Extract

Water

Wheat Extract And Flour

Wild Cherry Bark Extract

Wine and Wine Cherry

X

Xanthan Gum

3,4-Xylenol

Y

Yeast

Now, if this list does not blow your mind, nothing will!

CPSIA information can be obtained at www.ICGtesting.com
Printed in the USA
LVOW10s0048121214

418478LV00002B/3/P

9 781622 877416